Tell Me About
The World

WATERBIRD BOOKS

Columbus, Ohio

Children's Publishing

This edition published in the United States of America in 2004 by
Waterbird Books
an imprint of McGraw-Hill Children's Publishing,
a Division of The McGraw-Hill Companies
8720 Orion Place
Columbus, Ohio 43240-2111

www.MHkids.com

Library of Congress Cataloging-in-Publication Data is on file with the publisher.

Printed in China

ISBN 0-7696-3383-8

1 2 3 4 5 6 7 8 9 10 TOP 09 08 07 06 05 04

CONTENTS

THE ANIMAL KINGDOM   6

 THE PLANT WORLD   60

THE PREHISTORIC WORLD   100

 EARTH AND SPACE   132

OTHER FACTS   178

The Animal Kingdom

Contents

· · · · · · · · · · · · · · · · · ·

WHAT IS A SKUNK'S DEFENSE MECHANISM? 8
DOES AN OSTRICH REALLY BURY ITS HEAD IN THE SAND? 9

WHY DO MOSQUITO BITES ITCH? 10
WHY DO MOTHS EAT WOOL? 11

CAN ANIMALS UNDERSTAND ONE ANOTHER? 12
WHY DO PEACOCKS HAVE SUCH BEAUTIFUL TAILS? 13

HOW DO BIRDS SWIM UNDERWATER? 14
WHAT ARE ARMY ANTS? 15

WHERE DO ELEPHANTS LIVE? 16
WHY DO FLIES RUB THEIR LEGS TOGETHER? 17

WHAT IS A VAMPIRE BAT? 18
WHAT IS ANOTHER NAME FOR A DONKEY? 19

WHAT IS THE LARGEST ANIMAL IN THE WORLD? 20
WHERE IS A COBRA FOUND? 21

WHAT IS A GUINEA PIG? 22
DOES A COW REALLY HAVE FOUR STOMACHS? 23

WHERE DO RHINOCEROSES LIVE? 24
WHERE DO DOGS COME FROM? 25

HOW DOES A KINGFISHER CATCH ITS FOOD? 26
WHAT MAKES A MOLEHILL? 27

WHAT ARE CURLEWS AND GODWITS? 28
WHAT IS A MUTE SWAN? 29

HOW DOES A FLAMINGO EAT? 30
HOW DID THE GOLDEN EAGLE GET ITS NAME? 31

WHAT IS NATURAL SELECTION? 32
WHICH MAMMALS MIGRATE? 33

HOW DOES A CRICKET SING? 34
IS IT TRUE MALE SEAHORSES CAN BE MOTHERS? 35

WHY IS THE LION CALLED "KING OF THE BEASTS"? 36
WHY DO TIGERS HAVE DISTINCT COLORING? 37

WHAT IS A PANGOLIN? 38
CAN SQUIRRELS REALLY FLY? 39

WHAT IS AN AMPHIBIAN? 40
HOW DO FROG EGGS HATCH? 41

HOW DO BIRDS FLY? 42
HOW FAST CAN BIRDS FLY? 43

HOW DO SNAKES MOVE? 44
HOW DO SNAKES INJECT THEIR POISON? 45

HOW MANY KINDS OF FISH ARE THERE? 46
HOW CAN FISH BREATHE UNDERWATER? 47

HOW DOES A CATERPILLAR BECOME A BUTTERFLY? 48
HOW DO SPIDERS MAKE THEIR WEBS? 49

HOW DO BIRDS KNOW WHEN TO MIGRATE? 50
HOW FAR DO BIRDS MIGRATE? 51

WHEN IS THE BEST TIME TO SEE AN OWL? 52
WHEN DO WOODPECKERS PECK WOOD? 53

WHEN IS THE BEST TIME TO SEE A BAT? 54
WHEN DO BADGERS LEAVE THEIR SETS? 55

WHY DO HEDGEHOGS ROLL UP INTO A BALL? 56
WHEN DO ANIMALS HIBERNATE? 57

WHEN DO WHITE SEALS TURN DARK? 58
WHEN WILL WHALES BECOME EXTINCT? 59

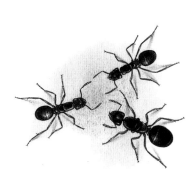
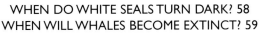

WHAT IS A SKUNK'S DEFENSE MECHANISM?

A skunk is a small, furry animal with distinctive black and white markings. When it is in danger or frightened, it sprays a disgusting-smelling liquid, called *musk*, at the threat.

The source of the spray is a pair of glands near the base of a skunk's tail. It can spray up to 12 ft. (4 m) with great accuracy. Before a skunk sprays, it raises its tail, growls or hisses, and stamps its front feet as a warning. If the spray gets into the skunk's victim's eyes, it may be blinded temporarily. The smell is so bad the victim can't breathe near it without choking. The smell can last for several days. Most animals learn to avoid skunks after just one or two encounters.

FACT FILE

Skunks are omnivorous, meaning they feed on both animal and vegetable substances. They primarily eat insects, small mammals and vertebrates, eggs, crustaceans, fruits, seeds, and some carrion. They search and dig in the earth, logs, and tree stumps for their food.

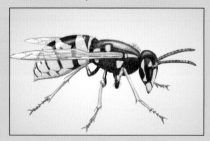

DOES AN OSTRICH REALLY BURY ITS HEAD IN THE SAND?

The ostrich is a large African bird. Myth has it that when it is scared, an ostrich hides its head in the sand. If danger comes close, the ostrich can't fly away, but it can run to escape. However, this can be tiring, so when an ostrich sees a threat at a distance, it sometimes lays on the ground and stretches its head out flat to make itself inconspicuous. It lies still until the threat goes away. If its nest is threatened, the ostrich will strike out with its powerful legs. It also uses these as a last defense if it cannot run any farther.

FACT FILE

The ostrich cannot fly to escape predators. It uses its remarkable speed as a means of defending itself. It can run for well over half a mile at up to 50 mph (80 kmh). This makes it the fastest runner in the bird world.

WHY DO MOSQUITO BITES ITCH?

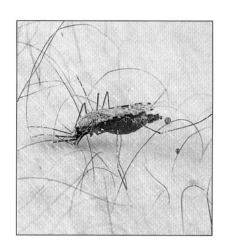 

The itchy welt that forms on the skin when a person has been "bitten" by a mosquito is, in fact, an allergic reaction to the insect's saliva. saliva injected into the skin prevents its victim's blood from clotting. A mosquito cannot actually bite because its jaws do not open. The middle of a mosquito's *proboscis* has six needle-like parts, called *stylets*. These are protected by the insect's flexible lower lip, or *labium*, most of the time. When a mosquito "bites," the lip slides out of the way like a sleeve as the stylets puncture the skin. The channels made by the stylets allow saliva to flow into the wound. This allows the insect to sip blood more easily. Only female mosquitoes bite. Only those of a few of the 3,000 or more species attack animals and people.

FACT FILE

Some of the worst diseases that people and animals suffer are spread by mosquitoes. Some species are carriers of such serious infections as Dengue fever, yellow fever, malaria, and filariasis.

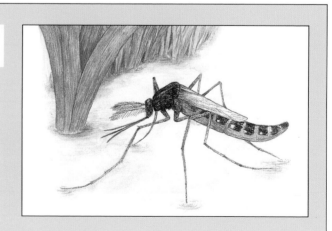

WHY DO MOTHS EAT WOOL?

Eyed hawk moth

Most people think that small moths, called "clothes moths," make moth holes in clothes by chewing them. It isn't adult moths that cause the problem, because they don't eat. It is the caterpillars that do the damage. A female moth lays its eggs on wool, or sometimes other fabrics. After 4 to 21 days, depending on the species, the eggs hatch into tiny caterpillars. There are various species of moths, including the webbing moth, the casemaking moth, and the tapestry or carpet moth. The casemaking moth caterpillar turns the wool it eats into a case. It lines the case with silk and drags it around. There it lives as a caterpillar until it turns into a pupa. Eventually it emerges as an adult.

FACT FILE

When at rest, eyed hawk moths resemble dead leaves. If alarmed, they open their forewings to reveal striking eye markings on their hind wings. This is likely to scare away predators, such as birds.

Death's head hawk moth

Poplar hawk moth

CAN ANIMALS UNDERSTAND ONE ANOTHER?

Howler monkeys

FACT FILE

Otters live in habitats where it is easier to use sound to communicate with each other rather than visual signals. As well as a warning growl, they use a variety of sounds such as chirps, chuckles, screams, growls, and squeals to express their feelings.

Although animals do not actually talk to one another, they do communicate by using signs and sounds. Humans use expressions, sounds, and gestures to indicate how they are feeling. Similarly, many animals make noises and signs to do the same thing. For example, mute swans, particularly males, will raise their wings, swim towards an intruder, and hiss to warn it off. Other birds sing both to attract mates and defend their territory. Howler monkeys actually howl to defend their territory. This acts as a warning as the sound carries through the forested areas of Venezuela. Animals can also communicate by using smell. Many mammals mark their territories with their scent.

WHY DO PEACOCKS HAVE SUCH BEAUTIFUL TAILS?

Two common expressions used to describe pride are "as proud as a peacock" and "as vain as a peacock." A peacock seems to take great pleasure in displaying its beautiful feathers. The display is done solely by a male to attract a female bird. A female, called the *peahen*, does not have these beautiful feathers. The most disctinctive feature of a male peacock is the trail of greenish feathers that grow from its back, not its tail. A male has a shiny, metallic greenish-blue breast and neck. Greenish feathers on its back lead to a train and dark purplish-blue underparts. During courtship, a male bird spreads its train into a magnificient fan as it parades in front of a female. It practically goes through a dance as it tries to attract the peahen.

FACT FILE

Indian peafowl, the proper name for the species of peacock shown below, originate from India and Sri Lanka. They can be found roaming in the wild.

HOW DO BIRDS SWIM UNDERWATER?

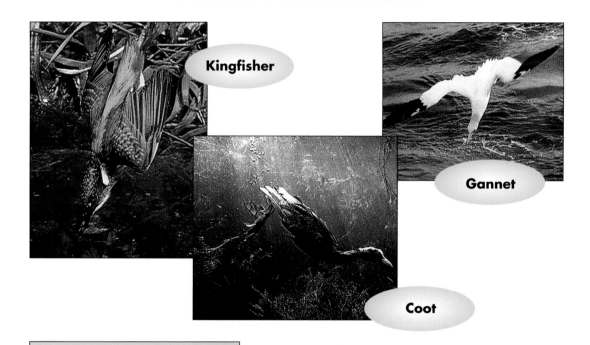

Kingfisher

Gannet

Coot

FACT FILE

A spoonbill is a long-legged wading bird that has a spoon-shaped bill. It swings its bill from side to side in the water to search for food.

Some wildfowl and seabirds can swim underwater, using various methods. Most, such as coots and cormorants, kick from the surface, point their heads down, and power themselves through the water with their strong legs. They often emerge some distance from where they dived. Birds like the gannet can swim underwater, as well as on the water's surface. Terns and kingfishers are among the birds that do not actually swim. They spot their prey from a height, plunge into the water and catch it, then float back up to the surface and take off. Gannets dive from heights of up to 130 ft. (40 m) and chase fish through the water. The masters of underwater swimming are the penguins. They seem to fly through water and can travel great distances.

WHAT ARE ARMY ANTS?

Wood ants

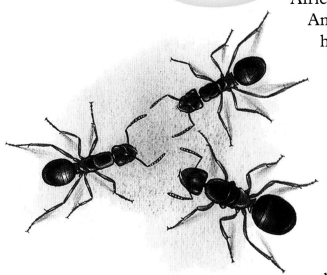

Army ants, which come from Africa and North and South America, are highly aggressive hunters. Like other ants, they live in colonies of between 10,000 and several million members. Their main prey are other insects and spiders. Some army ants also capture, kill, and eat other animals, such as small mammals or baby birds. A few ant species inhabit permanent nests and make raids through tunnels. Most species are nomadic and remain above ground all the time. Some ants hunt during the day, while others hunt at night.

Some kinds of army ant hunt and rest alternately for a few weeks. While active, they may cover great distances and take shelter in a new place every night. Once a queen has laid its eggs, however, ants will stay in one place for safety. They take shelter in large bunches, sometimes in a hollow tree or log. They can even be found hanging from a branch. The queen, eggs, and larvae are protected in the middle.

FACT FILE

Black ants have a special relationship with aphids. Black ants collect sweet honeydew from aphids. In return, aphids protect them from predators, such as ladybugs.

WHERE DO ELEPHANTS LIVE?

Wild elephants are found in only tropical Asia and sub-Saharan Africa, although their ancestors were much more widespread. After the last Ice Age, the climate got warmer, causing habitats to change rapidly. Woolly mammoths and many other species couldn't find sufficient food, and so they died out. Now only two species remain, The African elephant and the Asian elephant.

Unless provoked, elephants are gentle animals that can be trained. In Asia, they are still used as beasts of burden. Their great size and strength and their flexible trunks make them especially useful in industries such as forestry and logging. Their trunks consist of an adapted upper lip and nose that contain over 40,000 muscles. In parts of Africa, elephants have vast plains to roam naturally or in protected wildlife parks. Studies by zoologists have shown that elephants live in complex family groups, usually dominated by an older female.

FACT FILE

The ancestors of the elephant are known as *mammoths*. Their skeletons can be seen in museums. Their bones have been discovered in caves and river beds in North America and Europe.

WHY DO FLIES RUB THEIR LEGS TOGETHER?

Common housefly

A fly is an insect with one pair of large wings. There are thousands of different kinds of flies, including midges, gnats, horseflies, tsetse, and warble flies. The common housefly is among the best-known. A fly cleans itself by rubbing ts legs together. A housefly does not bite living animals. It is dangerous, however, because it carries bacteria that cause many serious diseases like typhoid fever, cholera, and dysentery. A housefly is a scavenger and eats by depositing a drop of digestive liquid on its food. This food may include garbage, rotten meat, animal dung, or uncovered food. Diseases can be transmitted on the fly's sticky foot pads and hairy body.

Greenbottle

Flesh fly

FACT FILE

Flies have an extremely keen sense of smell. A fungus called the *stinkhorn* contains a sticky, foul-smelling jelly which attracts flies. The flies eat the jelly and spread the spores when they fly away.

WHAT IS A VAMPIRE BAT?

Whiskered

Geoffrey's   **Natterer's**   **Bechstein's**

Several different kinds of bats in Central and tropical America are called *vampire bats.* At night, bats use their razor-sharp front teeth to bite warm-blooded animals, such as cattle, horses, and birds. Their saliva contains an anti-coagulant that prevents its victim's blood from clotting. A bat does not suck blood, but laps it like a cat. The vampire bat is named after the fictitious character Count Dracula, who sucked blood from people. Although bats have been known to attack sleeping humans, it is not common. One of the smallest of the bats is the common vampire bat, which is about 3 inches (8 cm) long and has reddish-brown fur on its body.

FACT FILE

Many species of bats live in colonies that may have thousands or even millions of members. Others live alone or in small groups. Most bats spend the day sleeping in their roost.

Long-eared bat

WHAT IS ANOTHER NAME FOR A DONKEY?

A male donkey is called a *jackass*. A female donkey is called a *jennet*. They are domesticated descendants of the wild ass of northern and northeastern Africa. They look like

zebras with no stripes, except for the legs on some. Donkeys are still commonly used in agriculture and as pack animals in southern Europe, southern Asia, and northern Africa. A donkey is about 4 ft. (1.2 m) high at the shoulders. Its coat is gray and slightly shaggy. One dark line runs along its back and another runs over its shoulders, making the form of a cross. Donkeys are known for their long ears and noisy bray.

FACT FILE

The result of a male donkey breeding with a female horse is a mule. These animals are hardy, very hard-working and resist disease better than donkeys. Unfortunately, all male mules and most female mules are sterile so offspring are rare.

WHAT IS THE LARGEST ANIMAL IN THE WORLD?

FACT FILE

The largest land mammal is the African elephant. It can weigh up to 6.9 tons (7 tonnes).

The blue whale is the largest and loudest animal on the earth. These enormous mammals eat tiny organisms, like plankton and krill. They sift their food through *baleen*, which is a horny substance attached to the upper jaw. Blue whales live in pods or small groups. These whales have 2 blowholes and a 2–14 inch (5–30 cm) thick layer of blubber. Blue whales are *rorqual* whales. They have pleated throat grooves that allow their throats to expand during the huge intake of water during filter feeding. Blue whales have 50–70 throat grooves that run from the throat to midbody.

WHERE IS A COBRA FOUND?

Cobras are found throughout the Philippines, southern Asia, and Africa. They are well known for their intimidating conduct and deadly bite. Cobras are recognized by their hoods that flare when they are angry or disturbed. The hoods are created by the elongated ribs that extend loose skin behind the cobras' heads.

The king cobra is the world's longest venomous snake. It averages 12 ft. (3.7 m) in length but has been known to grow over 18 ft. (5.5 m) long. It has olive or brown skin and bronze eyes. The king cobra is found in the Philippines, Malaysia, southern China, Myanmar (formerly known as Burma), India, Thailand, and the Malay Peninsula.

Cobras' venom often contains a powerful neurotoxin that acts on the nervous system. Venom has some medicinal uses. For example, some kinds of venom are used as painkillers in cases of arthritis or cancer.

FACT FILE

The spotted salamander is one of the larger members of the mole salamander family. It reaches almost 8 inches (20 cm) or more in length. It lays up to 200 eggs in a single mass in early spring, usually after the first warm rain.

King cobra

WHAT IS A GUINEA PIG?

Guinea pigs are South American plant-eating rodents. They are not related to pigs originally. They were an important source of meat for the Incas. Then, the Incas domesticated them. Groups of 5–10 wild guinea pigs spend daylight hours in shared burrows. They dig their burrows on grassy plains, in marshes, in forest margins, and in rocky areas. Occasionally, they take over abandoned burrows. Guinea pigs leave their burrow at night to eat. They are easily frightened. They utter shrill alarm calls whenever danger threatens and scamper back to their burrow.

In the wild, guinea pigs have long, coarse, gray or brown fur. Pet guinea pigs have been selectively bred for hair length and color. They may have smooth or wiry, long or short hair, which can be any combination of black, brown, rusty-red, or white. "Peruvian" guinea pigs have silky, long fur arranged in rosettes.

FACT FILE

The capybara is a South American rodent which is a close relative of the guinea pig. It is the largest of all rodents.

DOES A COW REALLY HAVE FOUR STOMACHS?

FACT FILE

Cows, sheep, and goats have no front teeth in their upper jaws. Instead, their gums form tough pads.

The simple answer to this question is no. A cow has only one stomach with four compartments, called the *rumen*, the *reticulum*, the *omasum*, and the *abomasum*. This complex system enables a cow to bring partly digested, softened food back into its mouth to be chewed and then swallowed again. This process is known as chewing the cud. Animals with these four-part stomachs are called *ruminants*. Micro-organisms in the digestive system allow animals to break down their food to obtain as many nutrients as possible. In the fourth compartment, the "true" stomach, gastric juices mix with the food, which then passes to the intestine for absorbtion.

WHERE DO RHINOCEROSES LIVE?

Rhinoceroses are found in Africa and Asia. The black rhinoceros and white rhinoceros live in Africa. The Indian, Javan, and Sumatran rhinos live in parts of Asia. Black, white, and Sumatran rhinos have two horns. The Indian and Javan species have only one horn. The horn is made of densely packed, coarse hair. It is used only in defense or in fights between males.

Rhinoceroses are vegetarians. They have to eat large amounts of grass and other plants every day to maintain their huge bodies. They usually move about very slowly to avoid wasting energy. They are distantly related to horses, but instead of hooves, they have three toes on each foot.

FACT FILE

Rhinoceroses are usually quiet and gentle, but if they feel threatened, they will charge. Despite their stubby legs, they can run remarkably fast – at speeds of up to 38 mph (48 kmh).

WHERE DO DOGS COME FROM?

Jack Russell terrier

All dogs, wolves, jackals, and coyotes are descended from a wolf-like creature called *tomarctus*. This ancient canine lived around 15,000,000 years ago. Its decendants belong to the branch of the dog family called *Canis*. These animals are so closely related to each other that they can breed and produce fertile offspring. Early man tamed wild dogs and trained them to hunt and retrieve. Images of dogs have been found on early cave paintings and rock art. Later, when people settled the land, they used dogs for herding and to guard property.

Some pet and working dogs do not look much like their wild relatives. However, they still think like them and regard their owners and families as members of their pack.

FACT FILE

Today, there are more than 400 recognized dog breeds, but they are all the same species. Breeders usually select the characteristics they want, and breed their dogs that exemplify that characteristic, such as a good coat, ears, strength, and so on.

Bulldog

HOW DOES A KINGFISHER CATCH ITS FOOD?

Kingfishers are birds with large heads, heavy, pointed bills; and stubby legs and tails. Some, like the common kingfisher, are brightly colored. Others, like the laughing kookaburra, are camouflaged.

A kingfisher may sit for hours on a branch beside the water looking for fish near the surface. Then, after hovering for a moment in midair, the bird dives for a fish. It either seizes the fish or spears it on its bill. The kingfisher bobs back to the surface and uses the membranes between its middle and outer toes to launch itself back into the air. Back at its perch, the bird tosses the fish into the air and swallows it headfirst. Other sources of food include crustaceans, frogs, and insects.

FACT FILE

Kingfishers burrow in the walls of riverbanks, sandbanks, or between the roots of upturned trees. They dig a tunnel about 3 ft. (1 m) long with a hollow at the end. There, the birds build a nest of fish bones on which to lay their eggs.

WHAT MAKES A MOLEHILL?

Molehills are small, cone-shaped mounds of soft earth that are often connected by slightly raised lines of earth. These mounds are made by moles. Each mound lies above one underground room of a mole's complicated home. The raised lines of earth are above the passages between individual rooms or runs where a moles digs for food.

A mole is a small mammal with a stocky, well-muscled body. With its large, strong forelegs and wedge-shaped head, it is perfectly adapted for its life burrowing through soil. A mole is

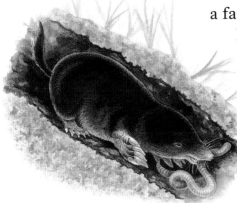

a fast, tireless digger. Its front paws have long, broad nails that turn outward, making them ideal for shoveling earth. Moles are almost blind, with tiny eyes, but they have excellent hearing. This enables them to locate their prey, such as earthworms and subterranean insects.

FACT FILE

The central chamber of a mole's home is larger than the other rooms. It contains a nest of leaves and grasses. Moles are born without fur but start to grow it after two weeks. They leave the nest after five weeks.

WHAT ARE CURLEWS AND GODWITS?

Black-tailed godwit

Curlew

FACT FILE

An avocet is another wading bird with a long, curved bill. The avocet feeds by opening its mouth slightly and sweeping it from side to side through the water. This is how it is able to collect and eat small animals. It also pecks at mud to find insects.

Curlews and godwits are long-billed, wading birds. The various species of curlew are long-legged birds that are related to sandpipers and snipes. They migrate vast distances between their winter feeding grounds and their summer breeding areas. For example, the curlew breeds in Siberia and winters as far south as the Philippines, Indonesia, and even Australia.

All curlews have long, slender bills which curve downward. They nest on dry ground, often far from water. They get their name from their eerie call.

The four species of godwits have bills that curve slightly upward. They nest in marsh- or grassland. The bar-tailed and black-tailed species nest in northern Europe. The marbled and Hudsonian species nest in northern North America.

WHAT IS A MUTE SWAN?

FACT FILE

Swans nest along the shores of rivers, waterways, and the coast in the summer. They move to large lakes in the winter. Mute swans feed mainly on underwater plants. They also graze on marshland during the winter.

Swans are waterfowl that are closely related to, and larger than, ducks and geese. A mute swan has an orange bill with a prominent black knob. It swims with its neck held in a graceful *S*-shape. Mute swans aren't, in fact, mute. They make snorting noises and hiss when they are threatened. When they are flying, their wings make a throbbing sound with each wingbeat.

In summer, breeding pairs are territorial. The males can be very aggressive in defense of their nest and cygnets. In winter, mute swans feed in large flocks. They feed by upending themselves and reaching down with their long necks to nibble underwater plants.

HOW DOES A FLAMINGO EAT?

A flamingo is a bird with long, stilt-like legs, a curved neck, and a large bill. When they feed, flamingos dip their heads under the water and scoop backwards with their heads upside down.

The edges of a flamingo's bill have tiny, narrow crossways plates called *lamellae*. The large, fleshy tongue pressing against the inside of the bill strains the water out through the lamellae, leaving behind small invertebrates and vegetable matter upon which this bird feeds.

All flamingos live in colonies. Some of these have tens of thousands of individuals. Flamingos mate yearly. Their nest consists of a mound of mud, built up to keep the egg from the water, with a shallow depression in the top. Flamingos build the mounds by scooping mud and smoothing it onto the pile with their bills. Each parent takes turns sitting on the single egg while the other parent feeds. Sitting on the egg serves to keep it warm in most areas. In hot areas like the lakes of the Rift Valley in Kenya, flamingos sit on the egg to keep it cool.

FACT FILE

Different flamingo species have slightly different coloring. Within a species, color varies according to geographic location and to what flamingos eat. For instance, flamingos that eat large amounts of pink crustaceans have brighter feathers than those that do not.

HOW DID THE GOLDEN EAGLE GET ITS NAME?

FACT FILE

The buzzard is a common sight in America. It can often be seen perching on telephone wires or poles, something an eagle would never do. A buzzard also can be seen circling above its nesting territory.

The golden eagle is North America's largest predatory bird. The plumage of an adult eagle is largely brown, darkening nearer to the wings. The tail is grayish-brown. The feathers at the eagle's head and nape of its neck are golden brown, hence its name.

The golden eagle is a supreme flier. Using the rising air on the sides of its mountain habitat, it rises and spirals high into the air, covering vast areas of ground. It can ride air currents between ridges and glide down at speeds of up to 120 mph (190 kph). Then, it swoops up gracefully to its next landing point. The golden eagle's flight is very graceful when it moves slowly in still air, or even when it battles strong winds. Occasionally, it dives vertically onto its prey. At times, its speed is said to rival that of the fastest falcons!

WHAT IS NATURAL SELECTION?

Natural selection is a process through which animals and plants evolve. Successful individuals tend to be those that are best suited to their environment. A mutation in genes also can play a part in this process. For example, mutation in genes could result in a giraffe with a longer neck than others in its group. The giraffe would be able to reach more leaves, thus becoming stronger and more likely to breed successfully and pass on its genes for a longer neck to its offspring. This would make them more successful in turn. Individual giraffes with genes that mutated to give them a shorter neck would be less able to find food, would go hungry, and would be less likely to breed. Thus the genes for short necks would eventually die out. The theory of natural selection is based on the great variation among even closely related individuals. In most cases, no two members of a species are exactly alike. Each member has a unique combination of traits such as size, appearance, and ability to withstand harsh conditions.

FACT FILE

In 1858, Charles Darwin and another British naturalist, Alfred R. Wallace, presented similar theories of natural selection. Many biologists rejected the idea at first.

WHICH MAMMALS MIGRATE?

Caribou

Many animals migrate, including birds, some whales, sharks, and butterflies. Similarly, mammals migrate, such as caribou and reindeer. Whether they are in the ocean or on land, animals migrate to find food and to breed. Humans and other animals have learned to take advantage of these annual cycles of movements. Crocodiles, for instance, lay in wait for the massive herds of wildebeest as they cross the rivers of the Great Plains of Africa.

Caribou live in herds in the cold northern regions of North America. In the summer, they feed on grass and shrubs on the tundra. When snows bury their food supply, caribou migrate south to warmer, forested regions where they eat lichen. Caribou return north when the snows start to thaw.

FACT FILE

The lemming is a small rodent, whose populations vary over roughly four years. At the peak, food is scarce, and lemmings are forced to migrate. According to legend, great numbers of lemmings throw themselves off cliffs and drown. It is more likely that they just starve.

HOW DOES A CRICKET SING?

Crickets are jumping insects that are related to grasshoppers. Species include the European house cricket and the common cricket of the United States. Crickets live in fields, meadows, and the grass alongside roads. Most songs are produced by the males, although females of some species sing as well. Unlike grasshoppers, which produce sounds using their legs, crickets do so by rubbing their front wings together. They do not have ears, but they hear using organs in their front legs. Cricket songs are mating calls that are designed to attract females. The songs usually consist of a series of chirps or a set of trills.

Cricket

Crickets differ from grasshoppers in other ways. Most crickets have wings that lie flat over each other on their backs, while those of grasshoppers are slightly raised. Most cricket antennae are longer than their bodies, unlike the short ones that grasshoppers possess.

Grasshopper

FACT FILE

A grasshopper is an insect that can leap about 20 times as far as the length of its body. If a human being had that same leaping ability, he or she could jump about 120 ft. (37 m).

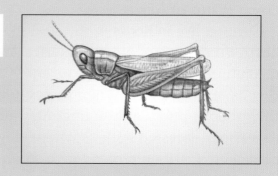

Is it true male sea horses can be mothers?

The sea horse is a small fish that got its name because of its horse-like face. Typically, the female of a given species bears offspring, but in sea horses it is the reverse. When the female sea horse lays its eggs, it puts them into the broad pouch beneath the tail of the male. When the young have hatched and are ready to leave the pouch, the mouth of the pouch opens wide. The male alternately bends and straightens his body in convulsive jerks. Finally, a baby sea horse is shot out. After each birth, the male rests. When all the babies are born, he shows signs of extreme exhaustion, including getting very pale in color.

FACT FILE

The sea horse has been described as having the head of a horse, the tail of a monkey, the pouch of a kangaroo, the hard outer skeleton of an insect, and the independently moving eyes of a chameleon.

WHY IS THE LION CALLED "KING OF THE BEASTS"?

Although lions are not all powerful, very few other animals will attack them. Thus, the lion has long been seen as a symbol of strength and referred to as "king of the beasts." Many kings and warriors, such as Richard the Lionheart, used the symbolism of the lion to emphasize their power. Lions used to be widespread. Two thousand years ago, they could be found in southern Europe. Today, almost all but a few of them live in Africa.

FACT FILE

Lions and tigers are thought of as the greatest cats of the wild. However, tigers and lions never meet in the wild. Lions are native to Africa, and tigers are native to Asia.

WHY DO TIGERS HAVE DISTINCT COLORING?

The tiger is one of the largest big cats. The base color of the tiger's coat is fawn to red. Tigers appear progressively darker the farther south they live. The Balinese tiger is the darkest. Underneath the tiger, its fur is white. Its coat has black to brownish-black stripes. These contrasting colors provide a wonderful camouflage for the tiger in its natural habitat.

FACT FILE

A leopard is another member of the big cat family. It has a remarkable coat. The name *leopard* is from the Latin word *leopardus* which means "spotted lion."

WHAT IS A PANGOLIN?

Pangolins are brown, scaly animals that resemble South American armadillos. Pangolins feed on ants. Like anteaters, they have no teeth but have long snouts and sticky, string-like tongues to catch the ants and termites on which they feed. Pangolins have overlapping horny scales to make a coat of armor. They roll themselves into heavily armored tight balls that are difficult for any predator to open.

Various species live in Indonesia, southeastern Asia, and parts of sub-Saharan Africa. They vary in length from 3 to 5 ft. (0.9 to 1.5 m). Their front feet have strong claws used for ripping open ant and termite nests to fish out insects. Their strong claws also are helpful for climbing trees.

FACT FILE

Although the Chinese pangolin climbs with agility, it feeds mainly on the ground. It uses its strongly clawed feet to dig for termites.

CAN SQUIRRELS REALLY FLY?

There is a kind of squirrel in southern Asia that can fly or, to be exact, glide. It has folds of skin between its front and back legs which, when stretched out, act like sails. The giant flying squirrel has a distinctive, thickly-haired flying membrane that extends from its wrists to its hind

legs. It is further expanded by a skin fold between the base of the tail and the hind legs. This membrane is composed of sheets of muscles that can be tensed or relaxed, enabling the squirrel to control the direction of its glide. In addition, there is a large spur on the edge of this membrane that helps to support it. Flying squirrels are nocturnal. This means they sleep during the day and become active at night.

FACT FILE

Ground squirrels are short-tailed, burrowing rodents that live in groups in open country, such as tundra, grasslands, and even alpine valleys. North American ground squirrels are closely related to chipmunks and prairie dogs. They are nervous and do not stray too far from the burrow.

WHAT IS AN AMPHIBIAN?

The internal organs of an amphibian

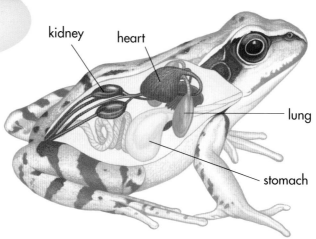

kidney

heart

lung

stomach

FACT FILE

Some brightly colored amphibians produce poison in glands on their skin. The bright colors warn birds and animals not to eat them. The poisons are among the most powerful known to human beings. In South America, poison from the poison arrow frog is added to the arrow tips used by the Indians for hunting.

Amphibians share characterisitcs with fish and reptiles. There are 4,400 living species of amphibian, including frogs, toads, newts, and salamanders. Many amphibians live mainly on land, but most spend at least some of their lives in water.

To a certain extent, frogs and salamanders are able to breathe through their damp skins, both in the water and on land. Toads must rely largely on their lungs and cannot remain in the water for long. Toads and frogs are similar in many ways, although toads usually have rougher, drier skins and may waddle rather than hop as frogs do. Some toad spawn is produced in strings, like necklaces, rather than in a mass of eggs like the frog. The largest amphibian, the Chinese giant salamander, is 6 ft. (1.8m) long.

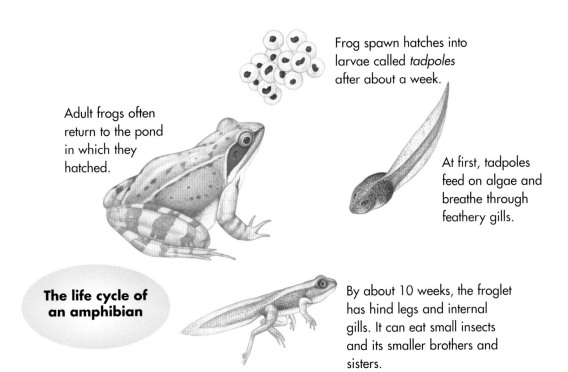

Frog spawn hatches into larvae called *tadpoles* after about a week.

Adult frogs often return to the pond in which they hatched.

At first, tadpoles feed on algae and breathe through feathery gills.

The life cycle of an amphibian

By about 10 weeks, the froglet has hind legs and internal gills. It can eat small insects and its smaller brothers and sisters.

HOW DO FROG EGGS HATCH?

Most amphibians lay their eggs in water. Frogs' eggs are called *spawn*. They are protected from predators by a thick layer of jelly. A tadpole develops inside this layer. When it hatches out, a tadpole is able to swim, using its long tail. It breathes through gills. As a tadpole grows, first hindlegs and then forelegs begin to grow. Lungs develop, and the young frog is able to begin to breathe with its head above water. Gradually, the tail shortens until the young frog resembles its adult parents.

FACT FILE

The tree frog lives in the rain forests of South America. It uses the pools of water in the center of certain tropical plants. Although it can swim, it spends much of its life out of water, among the leaves of trees where there are plenty of insects for food. It has sticky toes that enable it to climb.

HOW DO BIRDS FLY?

The bodies of birds are specially modified to give them the power of flight. Their bones are hollow to keep them light. Their bodies are also extremely lightweight, allowing them to glide and fly with minimum effort. For example, an eagle has a wing span of more than 7 ft. (2 m), and yet, it weighs less than 10 lb. (4 kg). Birds also have air sacs linked to their lungs to give them extra oxygen as they flap their wings.

Flying is a combination of gliding and powered flight. When a bird flaps its wings, the wings move in a complicated way, scooping air downwards and backwards. The wing actually twists so that the air is pushed back in the right direction to give lift. The wings are twisted again on the forward stroke so that they slide easily through the air without slowing down the bird's flight. A bird's feathers, which help reduce wind resistance in flight, are ideal because they are very light, yet also strong and flexible.

FACT FILE

The falcon is a bird of prey which feeds on other birds and small animals. It is equipped with powerful talons and a sharp beak. It uses these to kill and dismember its prey. When the falcon dives on its prey, it closes its enormous wings and drops like a stone to pick up speed. Powerful muscles in the bird's legs help to cushion the impact of the strike.

The internal organs of a bird

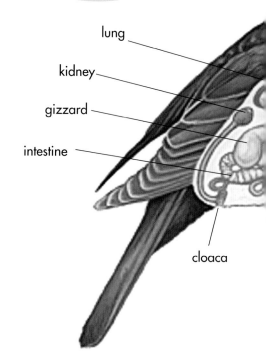

lung

kidney

gizzard

intestine

cloaca

HOW FAST CAN BIRDS FLY?

It is difficult to measure the speed of a bird in flight. They do not fly in straight lines, and their speed is greater if the wind is behind them or if they are diving. Not all experts agree on the published figures concerning the speed of various species of birds in flight.

In general, the heavier a bird is, the faster it needs to fly to stay in the air. It is believed that the fastest recorded flight for a bird was that of a homing pigeon flying at 94.2 mph (150.72 kmh).

A few speeds, however, are generally accepted. Some species of ducks and geese can fly about 63 mph (100 kmh). Peregrine falcons can fly at up to 75 mph (120 kmh), while hummingbirds reach speeds of 56 to 60 mph (90 to 95 kmh). Starlings are thought to fly at about 45 to 50 mph (70 to 80 kmh). Swifts can achieve almost 60 mph (95 kmh), and swallows usually fly about 25 mph (40 kmh), which helps them make their long migration flights quickly.

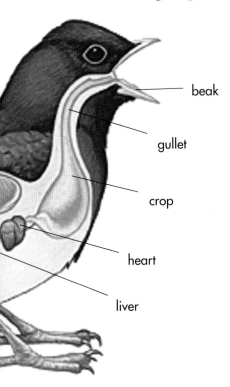

beak

gullet

crop

heart

liver

FACT FILE

Some birds cannot fly at all.
This includes penguins who
use their wings in water, enabling them
to swim very fast. The penguin shown below
is a rare yellow-eyed species. There
are only about 3,000 of
them left in the world.

The sidewinder

HOW DO SNAKES MOVE?

Snakes have several ways of moving. The most common way is for them to throw their bodies into loops and move forward by pressing against something solid.

Another way a snake moves is by contracting its muscles. This pushes the body along.

The desert-living sidewinder snake moves by throwing a loop out to one side. Then, it slides its body towards the loop while throwing another loop sideways at the same time. The sidewinder looks like a spring rolling along the sand, but this is an effective way of moving on this soft surface. Most snakes are able to swim effectively by using a wriggling motion.

FACT FILE

Snakes and crocodiles are both reptiles. A reptile is an air-breathing animal with a body structure between that of an amphibian and a mammal. Living reptiles include crocodiles, tortoises and turtles, snakes, and lizards.

HOW DO SNAKES INJECT THEIR POISON?

Some snakes have saliva glands that produce a toxin poisonous to their prey. This substance is called *venom*, so these snakes are described as being venomous. Some snakes' venoms are so powerful they could kill an elephant. About 200 venomous snakes worldwide (there are 412 species) are thought to be dangerous to people.

Among the most famous of these snakes are the cobras. Their fangs are at the front of the mouth, and the venom gland is farther back. The gland is surrounded by muscles that squeeze it when the snake bites. This forces the venom into the fang and down through the tip into the victim's flesh.

Another method of delivering venom can be seen in the African bird snake. This creature has massive fangs, with grooves running down one side, at the back of its mouth. Just above the grooves is a hole that leads from the venom gland. When this snake bites, venom drips through the grooves into the wound.

The cobra

FACT FILE

Giant snakes have been reported in many parts of the world. The largest recorded snake is the anaconda, which can reach a length of 30 ft. (9 m).

HOW MANY KINDS OF FISH ARE THERE?

Fish have existed for millions of years and have evolved into thousands of different types. There were fish in the oceans long before human beings appreared on the earth. Today, there are over 40,000 different kinds of fish. They inhabit every conceivable watery habitat on the planet.

Fish are divided into three general categories. Cartilaginous fish have skeletons made of flexible cartilage rather than rigid bone. Sharks, skates, and rays are included in this category. Bony fish, as their name suggests, have bony skeletons and are covered with scales of a similar substance. Members of this group of fish are the most common and account for over 90 percent of all fish. Lungfish are a special type of fish, because they have both gills and lungs. This category of fish includes mud skippers.

swim bladder

backbone

stomach

gills

heart

intestine

pelvic fin

Cross-section of a fish

FACT FILE

Salmon breed in small freshwater streams but spend most of their lives in rivers and seas. To breed, they return to the stream where they hatched. They even leap up waterfalls in order to reach their spawning grounds.

HOW CAN FISH BREATHE UNDERWATER?

Fish are able to breath underwater because they have special organs called *gills*. Gills are bars of tissue at the side of a fish's head. Gills have masses of finger-like projections that contain tiny blood vessels. Water goes into the fish's mouth and flows over its gills. The gill filaments take in oxygen, which is dissolved, from the water and pass it into the fish's blood.

In this way, the gills serve the same function as the lungs of air-breathing animals. If water is contaminated, fish need to take oxygen from another source. Some fish attempt to come to the surface of the water and take in oxygen from the air. However, their gills are neither suitable nor adept at processing oxygen from the air.

Fish are able to smell, although they do not use their gills for this. They have two small nostrils on their heads, which act as organs of smell. The sense of smell is much more developed in some fish than it is in others. Sharks, for example, use their keen sense of smell to hunt down and catch other animals to feed on.

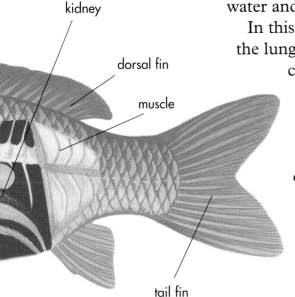

kidney

dorsal fin

muscle

tail fin

FACT FILE

Piranhas are very aggressive fish and can be dangerous in large numbers. Piranhas supposedly can strip all the flesh off of a pig or cow in a few minutes. They are probably not dangerous to human beings unless attracted to blood.

47

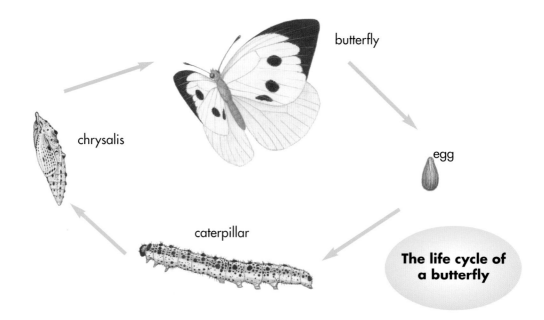

butterfly

chrysalis

egg

caterpillar

The life cycle of a butterfly

HOW DOES A CATERPILLAR BECOME A BUTTERFLY?

A female butterfly can lay from hundreds to thousands of eggs, depending on her species. If its offspring will eat only one type of plant, it will lay its eggs on that particular plant. After days or weeks, the eggs hatch into tiny grubs called *caterpillars*. They begin to feed and grow immediately, shedding their skins several times as they outgrow them.

When a caterpillar is fully developed and large enough, it spins a little button of silk onto a plant. It clings onto the plant with its rear end, dangles its head down, and shrugs off its skin. It then hardens to a pupa or chrysalis.

During the next weeks or months, or even over winter, the creature inside the hard shell changes completely. When it emerges, it is a butterfly. It spreads its wings so that they can dry and become firm before the butterfly will attempt to fly.

FACT FILE

This hover fly mimics a wasp, even though it has no sting. It is an excellent flyer, and can hover or fly backwards or sideways if necessary. It feeds on flower nectar.

HOW DO SPIDERS MAKE THEIR WEBS?

Spiders spin their webs from silk, which is pumped out from tiny nozzles at the back of the abdomen called *spinnerets*. As the spider stretches the silk into a thread, it hardens and becomes proportionately stronger than steel.

Some of these threads are quite sticky, while others simply support the web. The spider is able to feel the vibrations of the web when an insect flies into it. It then runs quickly across the web to capture its prey. Usually, the insect is wrapped in silk before being eaten by the spider.

FACT FILE

Ants are called *arthropods*. This means they have hard outer shells to protect their organs and joints to allow for free movement.

FACT FILE

Caribou usually live in relatively small numbers. But, when the time comes for them to migrate in search of food, they form herds of up to 3,000.

HOW DO BIRDS KNOW WHEN TO MIGRATE?

Migration is the movement of birds south from their summer breeding grounds to their winter feeding grounds in autumn and the return north in spring. Other forms of migration are the movement from inland to costal regions or between high and low ground.

Some birds fly to warmer regions because they cannot survive the cold. Others leave because their normal food is unavailable, and the birds would starve if they stayed. But how do birds actually know when to make this long flight? It is believed that birds can tell when the days get shorter in autumn and longer in spring. This acts as an "alarm clock" to tell birds that it is time to go. Some birds, such as migrating swans or geese, take the weather into account as well and stay at stopping-off points longer if conditions are suitable.

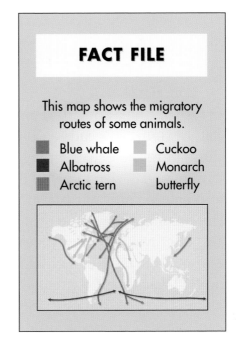

FACT FILE

This map shows the migratory routes of some animals.

■ Blue whale
■ Albatross
■ Arctic tern

■ Cuckoo
■ Monarch butterfly

HOW FAR DO BIRDS MIGRATE?

The champions among birds that migrate are the arctic terns. These amazing birds will travel as many as 22,000 miles (35,000 km) during the course of a year, going back and forth. They nest over a wide range from the Arctic Circle to as far south as Massachusetts. It will take these birds about 20 weeks to make their trip down to the antarctic region. The arctic terns average about 1,000 miles (1,600 km) a week.

Most land birds make only short journeys during their migrations. But there is one bird, the American golden plover, that makes a long, nonstop flight over the open ocean. It may fly from Nova Scotia directly to South America, a distance of about 2,400 miles (3,800 km), without stopping.

It is not certain that birds start and end their migrations on the same day each year. But, there is one bird that comes close to it. It is said that the famous swallows of Capistrano, California, are thought to leave on October 23 and return on March 19. However, their date of departure and arrival has been found to vary from year to year.

WHEN IS THE BEST TIME TO SEE AN OWL?

Owls are thick-bodied, rounded birds with large, flat, or rounded heads and legs. Owls are difficult to see because they are well-camouflaged, sleep mostly during the day, and emerge only at dusk or even later in the evening. They have evolved to suit this nocturnal life. They have extremely sensitive hearing. Their ears are set slightly off center, which allows them to pinpoint prey. They can focus their eyes accurately and instantly and open the pupils very wide to make use of what light is available. Owls have very soft plumage so that they can fly noiselessly and swoop down on to their prey of small mammals and insects.

FACT FILE

Many owls, such as the barn owl, are helpful to farmers because they eat mice, rats, and pests that eat crops. But, they were regarded for many years as birds of bad omen. Some people accuse them of eating domestic fowl.

WHY DO WOODPECKERS PECK WOOD?

FACT FILE

Most woodpeckers eat insects, but some feed on fruits and berries. Sapsuckers feed regularly on sap from certain trees in some seasons.

There are few birds that are as specialized as the woodpecker. They are rarely seen away from the trees that supply their food and nest sites. Woodpeckers are particularly known for their probing for insects in tree bark and chiseling nest holes in dead wood.

Most woodpeckers spend their entire lives spiraling up tree trunks in search of insects. In the spring, you can hear the loud calls of woodpeckers, often accompanied by drumming on hollow wood or occasionally on metal. These

Green woodpecker

are the sounds that are associated with the males marking their territories. Most woodpeckers are solitary or travel only in pairs.

The green woodpecker's tongue is long and sticky, with a barbed point. It probes into anthills, and drags out and swallows ants. When the tongue is not being used, it winds back, like a coiled spring, into a groove under the top of the woodpecker's skull.

WHEN IS THE BEST TIME TO SEE A BAT?

FACT FILE

A bat called the *pipistrelle* has adapted to warm cavity walls or hanging tiles in homes because their normal woodland habitat has been lost. Natural roosting places have become scarce.

Bats are most easily spotted on open ground near ponds and rivers at dusk. Insects hatch and fly from the water in large numbers, which attracts the bats. The bats catch the insects by a process known as *echolocation*. This is a technique in which an animal processes sounds and listens for the echoes reflected from surfaces and objects in the environment. From the information contained in these echoes, the animal is able to perceive the objects and figure out exactly where they are. Bats change their roosting places from season to season. They choose caves, old ice houses, and trees in which to hibernate. These places provide a constant temperature just above freezing.

WHEN DO BADGERS LEAVE THEIR SETS?

FACT FILE

Although foxes and rabbits have burrows, badgers usually make the largest and most obvious holes, leaving a faint, musky scent in the air. Their footprints can be seen in the ground or in the snow.

Badgers have distinctive black and white faces, with broad bodies on powerful, short legs. They live in colonies underground, called *sets*, and throw out large amounts of soil at the entrances to their tunnels. They emerge from their sets at dusk to forage for food. They prefer hilly areas on the edges of woods or thickets with well-worked soil.

They feed on earthworms and other small animals, fruits, cereals, and vegetables, using well-worn paths to their chosen fields or clearings. Badgers take care to keep their sets warm and clean. Damp bedding is thrown out and fresh, dry grass or straw is scratched up and gathered to replace it.

WHY DO HEDGEHOGS ROLL UP INTO A BALL?

FACT FILE

The porcupine is another mammal that uses its spines for defense. Porcupines are heavy, relatively short-legged rodents, mostly nocturnal and herbivorous by nature.

Although hedgehogs spend time in woodland scrub and cover, as their name suggests, they also spend time in well-cropped or cut grasslands that support the worms and insects that are their staple diet. Hedgehogs do not burrow but wrap themselves up in a thick covering of leaves to form solid hibernation nests under cover. They also hide breeding nests in similar places.

Hedgehogs roll themselves up into balls with spines to protect themselves from most predators. The spines are erect when they roll up, and these form a sharp defense. Born with soft, white spines, dark ones soon grow between these. Fleas, ticks, and lice live among these spines.

WHEN DO ANIMALS HIBERNATE?

FACT FILE

Some mammals, like bears and squirrels, do not really hibernate. They sleep more in the winter than in the summer, but do leave their dens to feed when they can.

The word *hibernate* comes from Latin meaning "winter sleep." Certain animals, such as hedgehogs, dormice, and some bats, hibernate during the winter. They hibernate to escape the severe weather conditions and because food is hard to find. Before the animals hibernate, they eat as much as they can to get enough body fat for the winter. Hibernation is not like ordinary sleep. During hibernation, animals' body temperatures decrease until they are only a little warmer than the air around the animals. Because the animals are not keeping themselves warm, they burn body fat very slowly. As a result, the animals need less oxygen, and their breathing and heart rate drops. When spring arrives, hibernating animals are awakened by increasing warmth and by hunger.

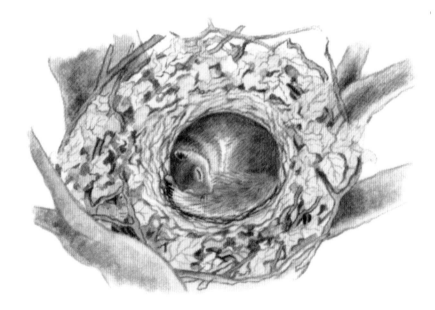

WHEN DO WHITE SEALS TURN DARK?

The common seal can be found on sandy waterways, bays, and rocky inlets away from the full force of the open sea. Although they live and feed in the water, they still come to the shore to breed and to molt. A seal pup is born with thick, white fur but loses this shortly after it is born. It will then be replaced by a much darker, sleeker coat. The seal's diet includes all kinds of seafood, such as fish, shellfish, crabs, and lobsters.

FACT FILE

A seal pup will suckle for ten minutes, five or six times a day. Its birth weight doubles in one week. After a month of rapid growth, the mother leaves to mate with another bull. The pup enters the sea to fend for itself.

WHEN WILL WHALES BECOME EXTINCT?

FACT FILE

The humpback whale was hunted almost to extinction, and its numbers dropped from 100,000 to 3,000 today. It is now generally protected.

Archaeological evidence suggests that primitive whaling, by Inuit and other peoples in the North Atlantic and North Pacific, was practiced from 3000 B.C. and has continued in remote cultures to the present day. All whale species are becoming less common because they have been regularly hunted for food and for oil. Other factors include environmental pollution and drift-net fishing. The gray whale was hunted almost to extinction by 1925 but was placed under complete international protection. It has increased in numbers since the 1940s. Some of the larger species of whales can be seen in Europe during their migration.

THE PLANT WORLD

CONTENTS

HOW DID FRUITS GET THEIR NAMES? 62
WHAT IS POISON IVY? 63

WHAT ARE SUCCULENTS? 64
WHAT IS DODDER? 65

CAN PLANTS FEEL? 66
WHICH PLANT APPEARS TO FLOAT ON WATER? 67

WHAT IS THE OTHER NAME FOR THE IRIS? 68
WHY IS HOLLY ASSOCIATED WITH CHRISTMAS? 69

IS THERE REALLY A FOUR-LEAVED CLOVER? 70
DOES BINDWEED ALWAYS TWIST IN THE SAME DIRECTION? 71

WHAT ARE GRAPES USED FOR? 72
WHO INTRODUCED THE DANDELION? 73

WHAT ARE CHANTERELLES? 74
WHICH IS THE LARGEST KNOWN FUNGI? 75

WHICH PLANT IS USED TO THATCH A ROOF? 76
WHAT IS THE FRUIT OF THE OAK? 77

WHY DO PLANTS NEED ROOTS? 78
WHICH PLANTS HAVE NO TRUE ROOTS? 79

HOW DO LEAF SHAPES VARY? 80
WHAT ARE BONSAI TREES? 81

WHY DO WE KISS UNDER MISTLETOE? 82
WHERE DID THE FIRST WILD STRAWBERRIES GROW? 83

HOW DID THE TIGER LILY GET ITS NAME? 84
WHAT ARE THE OLDEST PLANTS ON EARTH? 85

WHERE DOES THE WORD *LAVENDER* COME FROM? 86
HOW DID AROMATHERAPY DEVELOP? 87

WHAT IS MADE FROM THE WILLOW TREE? 88
WHAT IS BARK? 89

WHAT IS PEAT? 90
WHY DOES A PINE TREE HAVE CONES? 91

WHAT ARE STOMATA? 92
WHAT IS THE BIGGEST FLOWER? 93

HOW DO TREES GROW? 94
HOW DO LEAVES GROW? 95

HOW DO FLOWERS DEVELOP THEIR SCENT? 96
WHAT HAPPENS IN FLOWERS? 97

WHY DO PINE TREES STAY GREEN ALL YEAR? 98
WHAT ARE PERENNIAL PLANTS? 99

HOW DID FRUITS GET THEIR NAMES?

Many fruit names are derived from other languages, both historical and contemporary. Sometimes it is quite surprising to discover how certain names began. The root of the word *raspberry* lies in the German verb *raspen*. This means "to rub together" or "to rub as with a file" (or rasp), because the outside of this berry was thought to look like a file. The name *gooseberry* has nothing to do with geese but derives from the Saxon word, *gorst*, meaning "rough," because it grows on a rough or thorny shrub. Strawberries are not called this because gardeners keep them off the mud with straw. They are called *strawberries* because the runners stray all over the place. Strawberry is a corruption of the original "strayberry."

Melon is the Greek word for *apple*, while *tomato* is the Caribbean name for *love-apple*. Cranberry is a more recent word. They were once called "craneberries," because the slender stalks resemble the long legs and neck of a crane.

FACT FILE

Botanists classify tomatoes as fruits. Horticulturists, however, classify them as vegetables. Most other people consider tomatoes to be vegetables because fresh tomatoes are used in much the same way as many other vegetables.

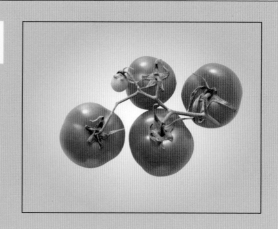

WHAT IS POISON IVY?

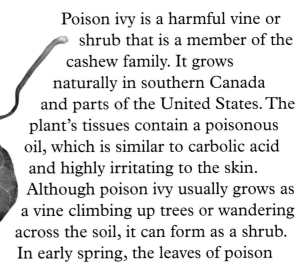

Poison ivy is a harmful vine or shrub that is a member of the cashew family. It grows naturally in southern Canada and parts of the United States. The plant's tissues contain a poisonous oil, which is similar to carbolic acid and highly irritating to the skin. Although poison ivy usually grows as a vine climbing up trees or wandering across the soil, it can form as a shrub. In early spring, the leaves of poison ivy are red. By late spring, they change to shiny green. Then, in autumn they turn back to red or orange. Each leaf is composed of three leaflets with notched edges. Later in the season, clusters of whitish, waxy fruits that resemble berries form. These are just as poisonous as the leaves.

FACT FILE

Ground ivy is a member of the mint family and is not closely related to true ivies or poison ivy. It has a trailing habit and sends creeping stems across the ground. It also forms mats of leaves where it takes root.

WHAT ARE SUCCULENTS?

Cacti

FACT FILE

Cacti have many rare and beautiful features, developed during a long and slow evolutionary process. One of their principal characteristics is the ability to adapt to harsh conditions that would cause most other plant groups to perish quickly.

Succulents are plants that have organs such as leaves, stems, or roots. These organs are capable of storing water in order to survive extended periods of drought. All the plants in the cactus family are considered to be stem succulents. During periods of moisture, the stem swells and then during droughts, it slowly contracts. Cacti that have ribs are particularly well adapted to this because the ribs fill in and contract like an accordion. Cacti get their name from the Greek word *kaktos* meaning "thistle."

WHAT IS DODDER?

Dodder is a strange, totally parasitic plant. When their tiny seeds start to grow, they put up thin threads that begin to twist in ever-increasing circles. Most seedlings die, because they fail to find the right sort of plant from which to take their food. If one seed finds the right host, it quickly attaches itself and pushes absorbing organs into the plant. The root of the seed then withers and dies, since the dodder plant has now taken all of its food from the host. The most popular host plants are alfalfa, clover, and flax. Dodder has tiny, pink leaves that have no need for chlorophyll, which enables most plants to make food from sunlight. In late summer, dodder produces small, pink flowers and then masses of tiny seeds.

FACT FILE

Once dodder has established itself, it produces a mass of pink threads which cover the host plant and greatly weaken it.

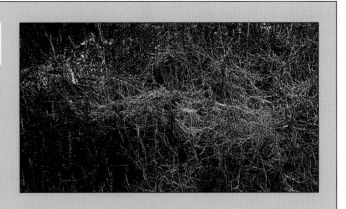

CAN PLANTS FEEL?

Although plants do not have feelings in the same way that we do, they can certainly respond to different stimuli. They are able to grow towards a light source, even if turned upside down. Some plants have very sensitive leaves, which will fold up if touched. Others have leaves that open and close according to the time of day. The Venus flytrap has sensitive leaf tips. When an insect lands on tiny hairs on the leaf, the pairs of leaves snap shut, trapping the insect inside. Plants are even able to perspire. Although you cannot see this happening, if you were to place a plant inside a plastic bag and fasten it, after a while you would see drops of

FACT FILE

Some plants have sensitive hairs on their leaves. If an unsuspecting insect lands on these sticky hairs, it soon finds its legs hopelessly entangled.

water form on the inside of the bag. The moisture you see comes from the leaves of the plant.

Lords and ladies

WHICH PLANT APPEARS TO FLOAT ON WATER?

A water lily, also called *pond lily*, is an aquatic plant with leaves that appear to float on water. The lily does, in fact, have roots in the water at the bottom of the pool. The white-flowered water lily is most commonly found in the wild. Its flowers may reach 1 ft. (30 cm) in diameter. Its fruits, when ripe, look like old brandy bottles. The green leaves are kidney-shaped and usually float on the surface of the water. But they may be submerged, especially while they are growing. Then, the flowers rise above the water on long flower stalks. Some kinds bloom during the day and others at night. Cultivated varieties come in every size and color.

FACT FILE

Yellow water lilies grow in lakes, ponds, and rivers. Bulrushes grow in marshes or in shallow water. They have tough stems that are round or triangular and up to 12 ft. (3.7 m) tall. Their tiny flowers are clustered into small, brownish spikes at or near the tops of the stems.

WHAT IS THE OTHER NAME FOR THE IRIS?

Fleur-de-lis is an alternative name for the iris and is French for "flower of the lily." It has a long history of use in royal symbolism, first appearing on a pharaoh's baton in 1,500 B.C. It was also adopted as the emblem of the kings of France in the 12th century. The name comes from the name of the Greek goddess of the rainbow, who was called *Iris*. Their three-part shape makes members of

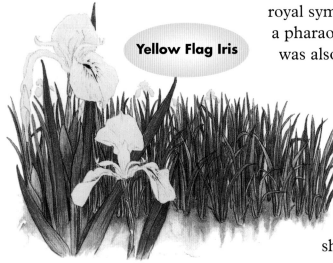

Yellow Flag Iris

the iris family easy to recognize. There are thousands of varieties, but they all have three sets of three petal-like parts: the lower part or falls, the upper part or standards, and the curved stylebranches in the middle, covering the stamens.

FACT FILE

King Charles V of France was the first ruler to adopt a design of three golden *fleurs-de-lis* on a blue background (technically known as a *field*) as his coat of arms in the 1300s.

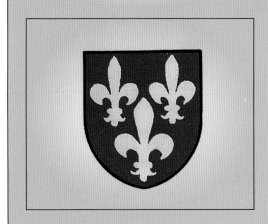

WHY IS HOLLY ASSOCIATED WITH CHRISTMAS?

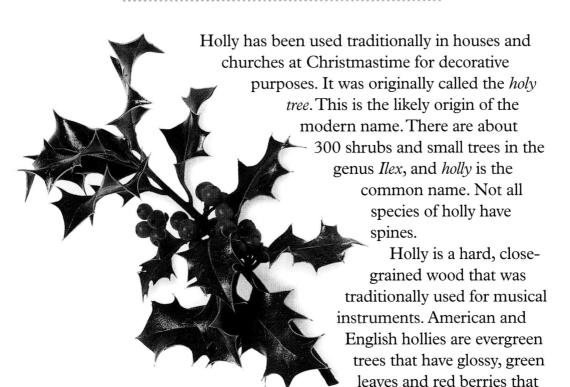

Holly has been used traditionally in houses and churches at Christmastime for decorative purposes. It was originally called the *holy tree*. This is the likely origin of the modern name. There are about 300 shrubs and small trees in the genus *Ilex*, and *holly* is the common name. Not all species of holly have spines.

Holly is a hard, close-grained wood that was traditionally used for musical instruments. American and English hollies are evergreen trees that have glossy, green leaves and red berries that are used to make colorful Christmas wreaths. The holly berries, which are actually fruits, are poisonous to human beings.

FACT FILE

The poinsettia is a popular houseplant also used as a Christmas decoration. What look like the bright red petals are actually a kind of leaf. The real flowers are the tiny green dots in the middle.

IS THERE REALLY A FOUR-LEAVED CLOVER?

A particular feature of the clovers is their three-lobed, or *trifoliate*, leaves. The "lucky" four-leaved clover can be found, but it is rare. Clovers are members of the pea family. There are around 250 species of true clover, including the white, red, crimson, and strawberry.

Clovers are generally plants of grassland, but they commonly grow near the coast and on chalky or clay soils. Red clover has been used for centuries in crop rotation as it puts nitrogen back into the soil. Today, it is used extensively as an animal food and soil-improving crop throughout Europe and northern and central North America.

FACT FILE

Clover flowers are very rich in nectar as a means of attracting insects. The white base of the flower tastes of fresh honey.

DOES BINDWEED ALWAYS TWIST IN THE SAME DIRECTION?

It is an interesting fact that all bindweed plants twist around their supporting plant in the same direction–counterclockwise–whichever way they begin. The Greater Bindweed, or Hedge Convolvulus, is a hedge plant found abundantly throughout England and Scotland. Despite the beauty of its flowers, bindweed is regarded as a pest by farmers and gardeners. Its roots are long and form a dense mass that consumes the soil. Its twisting stems extend in masses over all other nearby plants, thereby strangling them.

FACT FILE

If a gardener were to turn it in another direction, the bindweed, if unable to free itself and assume its natural direction from right to left, will eventually perish.

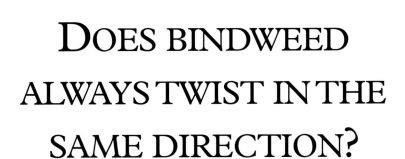

WHAT ARE GRAPES USED FOR?

Grapes are juicy, smooth-skinned berries that grow in clusters on woody vines. They have been cultivated for wine and food for thousands of years. Different varieties produce different colored berries, including black, green, purple, red, and white.

Four-fifths of the world's grapes are used for making wine. The main producers of wine are France, Italy, Spain, Portugal, Hungary, Bulgaria, Germany, the United States, Australia, New Zealand, Chile, and Argentina.

In the past, dried raisins were traded extensively because they could be transported without going bad.

FACT FILE

Most wine grapes are picked by machine. However, special grapes for making rare wines are carefully picked by hand.

72

WHO INTRODUCED THE DANDELION?

FACT FILE

When the flowers of the dandelion mature, they form feathered, cottony seeds that the wind carries far away.

The dandelion is a bright-yellow wild flower that grows in lawns, meadows, and on grassy verges. It is an irritating weed to gardeners because it is difficult to get rid of. The dandelion was imported to America by early colonists from Europe. It has smooth, coarsely-notched leaves. The notches are supposed to look like teeth. The dandelion's common name derives from the French *dent de lion*, meaning "lion's tooth." The golden-yellow head is really a composite flower. The stem is straight and hollow, and the milky white juice that exudes if you break it tastes foul. The long, thick root is pointed and has hair-like branches growing from it. It is these that break off in the ground and give rise to new plants if they are not removed. The dandelion reproduces by forming fertile seeds that need no pollination from other plants.

WHAT ARE CHANTERELLES?

Chanterelles are mushroom-like fungi with funnel-shaped caps. The delicious and fragrant golden chanterelle is a delicacy prized by gourmets. Chanterelles are known by the form of their spore-producing surface, which is smooth and veined.

Mushrooms are important to our environment because they help keep soil fertile for plants to grow. As mushrooms grow, they break down the dead material that they feed on, such as old leaves. Then, they release nutrients back into the soil that the plants can use again in future.

Many insects and small mammals eat mushrooms because they are an important source of nutrients.

Golden chanterelle

Trumpet chanterelle

FACT FILE

The term *tooth-fungi* covers a range of unrelated species that all have spines or teeth on which spores are produced. Because of pollution, many of these are becoming rare.

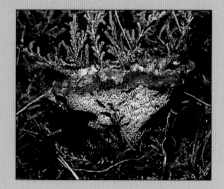

WHICH IS THE LARGEST KNOWN FUNGUS?

The giant puffball is the largest known fungi. It can grow as large as 5 ft. (150 cm), although an average fruiting body is the size of a football. Just one fruiting body produces about 7 trillion spores. The puffballs are ball-shaped fungi, and they are any shade of white to tan. They range in size from smaller than a golfball to larger than a basketball. When a puffball matures, its spores become dry and powdery. If touched, the puffball breaks open, and the spores escape in a smoke-like puff.

Black bovista

Scaly meadow puffball

FACT FILE

Flies and other insects are attracted to the stinking, slimy spore mass of the common stinkhorn. When they fly off after feeding, they carry away spores stuck onto their bodies. This is how the stinkhorn spreads to new locations.

WHICH PLANT IS USED TO THATCH A ROOF?

The material normally used to make roofing thatch is common reeds, which are tall grass-like plants. They grow in almost all temperate and warm regions. They are found in a variety of habitats, including low upland meadows, wet lowlands, and shallow lakes and ponds. Reedmarsh is a valuable wildlife habitat if managed properly. Usually the reeds are cut in the autumn, arranged into dense bundles, and laid in layers on roofs. The thatch is waterproof and provides good heat insulation for the house. If laid and maintained correctly, a thatched roof should last for up to 40 years. Traditionally, the bundles are held in position with pegs made from strips of willow, although chicken wire is commonly used now to help keep the reed in place.

Common reed

FACT FILE

In many wetland areas, reeds spread rapidly, crowding out other types of marsh grass. For this reason, it has to be cut down regularly. Reed grass has been used in the production of paper.

WHAT IS THE FRUIT OF THE OAK?

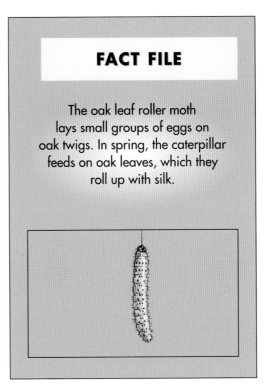

Oaks mature slowly and usually will not flower until they are about 20 years old. They live a long time, many for 200 to 400 years. The fruit of the oak tree is called the *acorn* and is an egg-shaped nut in a small cup. In spring, oaks produce small, yellowish-green flowers. Large amounts of windborne pollen are produced by the male flower clusters. The fertilized female flower starts off green and turns brown by autumn. Depending on the exact species, acorns range in length from under one-half in. (13 mm) to more than two in. (51 mm).

FACT FILE

The oak leaf roller moth lays small groups of eggs on oak twigs. In spring, the caterpillar feeds on oak leaves, which they roll up with silk.

WHY DO PLANTS NEED ROOTS?

Roots are not as attractive as leaves and flowers, but plants could not live without them. Anchored in the soil, they hold plants upright against wind and weather. They also grow out and down in search of water and minerals that are drawn all the way up to the leaves. Because trees grow to such enormous

heights, the roots need to grow outward to balance the spread of the branches above. Most roots grow in the top 1 ft. (30 cm) of soil. This part contains most of the minerals the tree needs to survive. Every single root grows a mass of tiny hairs near its tip to enable it to absorb water from the soil. There are little pockets of air in the soil. Without these, roots would wither and die.

FACT FILE

There is one plant that survives without roots, the Spanish moss. It grows in subtropical climates where the air is very wet. It absorbs all the moisture it needs through its fine, thread-like leaves.

WHICH PLANTS HAVE NO TRUE ROOTS?

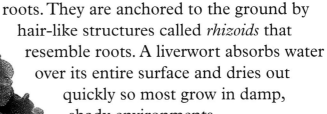

Liverwort

Liverworts, hornworts, and mosses do not have true roots. They are anchored to the ground by hair-like structures called *rhizoids* that resemble roots. A liverwort absorbs water over its entire surface and dries out quickly so most grow in damp, shady environments.

Moss has a short stem that grows from the rhizoids. It is covered by tiny leaves in a spiral pattern. The leaves contain chlorophyll, a green substance the plant uses to make food. In many cases, a vein runs the length of the leaf from the stem to the tip. This vein, called the *costa* or *midrib*, strengthens the leaf and carries food and water. Many mosses grow in moist or aquatic environments. Certain mosses, though, can survive extremely dry conditions. Their need for water changes with the amount of water available in the environment.

Other plants that do not have roots include lichens and air plants. Air plants cling to larger plants and absorb nutrients from rainwater.

FACT FILE

Lichens have no roots. They have an outer layer of fungal cells that are pigmented green, brown, or yellow. This protective layer, called the *upper cortex*, covers an area of green or blue-green algal cells.

Moss

HOW DO LEAF SHAPES VARY?

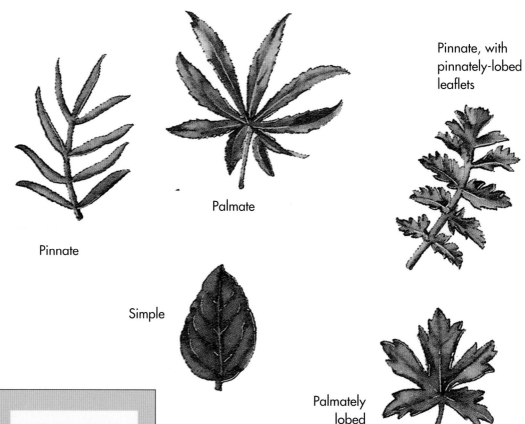

Pinnate, with pinnately-lobed leaflets

Palmate

Pinnate

Simple

Palmately lobed

FACT FILE

Some plants have all their leaves in a ring at the base of the stem. This is known as a *rosette*.

The shapes of plant leaves vary considerably. The edges of leaves may be smooth or jagged. The leaf blades may be undivided (simple), or they may be divided (lobed) in various ways. Some leaves may be made up of separate leaflets. The most common types of leaf shape are shown above.

The leaves themselves may be arranged on the plant in different ways, which is usually standard for any given type of plant. A leaf arrangement which has single leaves at each level is called *alternate*. Leaves arranged in pairs are called *opposite*. Opposite leaves may all face the same way, or each pair may be at right angles to the pair below.

80

WHAT ARE BONSAI TREES?

Bonsai trees are decorative miniature trees or shrubs. The art originated in China over 1,000 years ago. Then, trees were cultivated in trays, wooden containers, and earthenware pots, and they were trained in naturalistic shapes. Bonsai trees, though, have been pursued and developed primarily by the Japanese.

They are dwarfed by cutting their roots and branches, and training branches by tying them with wire. Some of these trees are very old and are perfect miniatures, even producing tiny flowers or cones.

FACT FILE

The Japanese are known for their ornate plants and gardens. Even as far back as 700 A.D., the Japanese developed beautiful gardens to enjoy.

WHY DO WE KISS UNDER MISTLETOE?

Early Europeans used mistletoe as a ceremonial plant. The custom of using mistletoe at Christmastime may date back to such practices. In many countries, tradition says that someone caught standing beneath mistletoe must be kissed.

Mistletoe is a parasitic evergreen plant with strap-like, leathery leaves that have curved ends. Mistletoe may be parasitic to the apple, fir, hawthorn, lime, oak, poplar, and sycamore trees. The mistletoe's tiny, yellow flowers appear in February and March. The berries appear in autumn and are ripe by midwinter. Mistletoe is associated with many holidays, especially Christmas. Legend says that the Druids cut mistletoe from the sacred oak for people to wear as charms. Teutonic mythology reports that an arrow of mistletoe killed Balder, son of the goddess Frigg.

FACT FILE

Although mistletoe is poisonous to human beings, it is a useful source of nutrition for birds in winter. The seeds stick to the birds' bills and are spread when birds sharpen their bills against the bark of trees.

WHERE DID THE FIRST WILD STRAWBERRIES GROW?

FACT FILE

Strawberries grow wild or are raised commercially in almost every country. Plant breeders have developed hundreds of varieties of strawberries that are suited for different growing conditions.

Wild strawberries first grew in ancient Rome. The first known hybrid was not developed until the 18th century in France, by crossing varieties from different regions of the Americas.

Strawberries are members of the rose family and are low-growing plants that usually spread by their extensive runners, from which roots extend into the soil. They are not classified as true berries because the small yellow "seeds" on the outside of the strawberry are, in fact, a separate fruit. The "berries" are pale green when first formed and slowly turn red once they are fully grown.

HOW DID THE TIGER LILY GET ITS NAME?

The tiger lily is a tall, hardy garden plant named after the black-spotted, reddish-orange petals of its flowers, which resemble the stripes on a tiger's skin. The tiger lily has spread from China, Japan, and Korea to become a popular garden plant in Europe and North America. A few varieties have red, white, or yellow petals.

Tiger lilies have greenish-purple or dark brown stems, which may grow from 4 to 5 ft. (1.2 to 1.5 m) tall and bear more than 15 flowers each in ideal conditions.

Tiger lily plants grow from bulbs and reproduce in an unusual way, by developing little black buds in the joints between the spear-shaped leaves and the stalk. When the buds are mature, they drop off the stalk to produce new plants near the mother plant.

FACT FILE

Magnolia trees are one of the oldest flowering plants. They are thought to have existed for over one hundred million years.

WHAT ARE THE OLDEST PLANTS ON EARTH?

Ferns are among the oldest kinds of plants that live on land. Scientists believe that ferns appeared on earth more than 350 million years ago. They do not have seeds, but they undergo a two-stage reproduction method. First, microscopic spores are produced on the underside of a mature plant's leaves. Once the spores are ripe, they drop off the leaves and are carried by the wind. If they land in a damp area, they sprout and grow into minute flat plants with small reproductive structures. Sperm fertilizes the egg, which begin to grow as the tiny plant shrivels and dies, and a new fern begins to develop.

FACT FILE

Tree ferns are among the oldest types of plants to exist. Many of them have no root systems and absorb moisture through the tops of their trunks.

WHERE DOES THE WORD *LAVENDER* COME FROM?

The word *lavender* comes from a Latin word that means "to wash." It is believed that this name may have been used because the ancient Romans scented their bathwater with it. The plants are native to Mediterranean countries and are members of the mint family.

The pale-purple flowers grow in clusters around the

top of a rigid stem. Lavender has long, narrow, gray-green leaves. Cultivated types of lavender include white and French, which has two little tufts at the top of the flower and is a deeper purple. Dried lavender retains its scent for a long time and is used in both potpourri and herbal pillows because it is thought to aid sleep.

FACT FILE

The petals of certain flowers contain sweet-smelling oils. Such flowers include jasmines, mimosas, and roses. The oils obtained from the petals of these flowers supply the fragrances for many high-quality perfumes.

Potpourri

How did Aromatherapy Develop?

Aromatherapy as an art and practice has been traced back to only around 5,000 years ago, though its roots are probably as old as the discovery of fire. It was the ancient Egyptians who first worked to perfect the practice of aromatherapy. They thought that plants which could produce such healing results must be gifts of their gods and hence incorporated aromatherapy into their religious ceremonies.

These ancient peoples used to perform sacred ceremonies in worship to their gods, burning incense and anointing their bodies with precious oils. Large quantities of aromatics were burned in public places to purify the air and drive away "evil spirits," which today may be considered emotional distress or illness.

FACT FILE

In ancient Africa, people discovered that when they rubbed plants on their skin, the oils that these plants left behind provided greater protection from the sun. Additionally, these oils helped to prevent skin problems and helped maintain softness.

87

WHAT IS MADE FROM THE WILLOW TREE?

Usually, willow trees live in moist habitats, floodplains, and riverbanks, where they grow very rapidly. Their wood is used in many ways, and their leaves supply food for wildlife. Twigs of the common osier are grown to use for basketmaking, and the light but dent-resistant wood of other willows is used for artificial limbs, wooden shoes, and baseball bats.

Willow bark contains the active compound *salicin*, which is used in many folk medicines. Aspirin is a derivative of salicylic acid, which was first produced from derivatives of willow bark.

FACT FILE

Willow-pattern china originated in Staffordshire, England, around 1780. Thomas Minton, then an apprentice potter, developed and engraved the design, taken from an old Chinese legend.

WHAT IS BARK?

Bark is the outer covering of the stem of woody plants, composed of waterproof cork cells. This outer bark protects a layer of food-conducting tissue called the *phloem*, *inner bark*, or *bast*. As the woody stem increases in size, the outer bark of dead cork cells gives way. It may split to form grooves, or shred, as in the cedar; or peel off, as in the sycamore. A layer of reproductive cells called the *cork cambium* produces new cork cells to replace or reinforce the old ones. Trees are sometimes damaged by animals that eat the outer bark by cutting through the phloem tubes. This can result in starvation of the roots and, ultimately, the death of the tree. The outer bark of the paper birch was used by Native Americans to make baskets and canoes.

FACT FILE

Bottle corks are made from the thick, spongy bark of the cork oak, which grows in the Mediterranean region. Because oaks produce durable, tough wood they are a good source for lumber.

WHAT IS PEAT?

In swamps and marshes, particularly in cold or temperate climates, matter that has fallen from dead plants decays slowly because there is little oxygen. Peat is partly decayed plant matter made up of layer upon layer of plants such as reeds, rushes, and sedges.

In Ireland, peat is used to generate electricity because other sources, such as coal, are scarce. Depending on its state of decay and the plants involved, dried peat ranges from a light yellow-brown tangle of plant matter to deep layers of dark brown, compact material that looks like brown coal. Commercially dug peat is removed by machine and used for various purposes. Black peat is used as a fertilizer and light brown peat as bedding for cattle and sheep. Moss peat, which comes mainly from sphagnum moss is used in agriculture as litter for poultry and horses, as well as a mulch and a soil conditioner. Efforts are being made to find alternatives because much of the peat bogs are being destroyed.

FACT FILE

Peat is the earliest stage of transition from compressed plant growth to the formation of coal. The oldest coal was formed 350 million years ago, and the process still continues in swamps and bogs.

Sphagnum moss

WHY DOES A PINE TREE HAVE CONES?

A pine tree has cones in order to reproduce. The pine cone is actually a highly modified branch that takes the place of a flower. Separate male cones and female seed cones are borne on the same tree. Each of the numerous scales of the male cone bears pollen, while each female cone scale bears ovules in which egg cells are produced. In the pine, the male cones are small and short-lived, and are borne in clusters at the top of the tree. At the time of pollination, great numbers of pollen grains are released and dispersed by the wind. Those that land accidentally on female cone scales extend pollen tubes part way into the ovule during one growing season. Usually, they do not reach the stage of actual fertilization until the next year. The cones that are usually seen are the seed cones, which are normally hard and woody.

FACT FILE

Scotch pine trees need to be tough to survive long, cold winters. They have thousands of tiny, needle-like leaves. The needles have a waterproof coating to protect them from the rain and snow.

WHAT ARE STOMATA?

Stomata are tiny holes in leaves, which the plant can open and close. When the stomata are open, they let air in and out, and water out. When the stomata are closed, water cannot escape from the leaves.

Plants absorb water from the soil through their roots. This water moves up the stem to the leaves, where about 90 percent evaporates through the stomata. Large trees lose more than 200 gallons (800 l) of water from their leaves each day. This loss of water from leaves by evaporation is called *transpiration*. Other plant processes that involve water include photosynthesis, which uses water to make food, and respiration, in which water is produced. When it is dark, plants shut down for the night by closing stomata.

FACT FILE

Every day, a large tree loses enough water for a person to take eight long showers. About 90 percent of the water absorbed by the roots is lost by the leaves in transpiration.

92

WHAT IS THE BIGGEST FLOWER?

FACT FILE

Green algae are the smallest plants. They form, for example, a greenish film often found on the bark of trees. Millions of cells of algae are needed to cover a tree trunk.

The biggest flower is called the *rafflesia*, a parasitic plant that does not photosynthesize. It grows in the rainforests of southeast Asia. The plant actually grows underground and is not visible until a large bud appears, somewhat like a cabbage. This opens up into a leathery flower which is approximately 3 ft. (1 m) across and weighs up to 22 lbs. (10 kg). The flower looks and smells just like a large pile of rotting flesh. It attracts thousands of flies, which pollinate the flower as they walk on it.

HOW DO TREES GROW?

Tree trunks consist of a number of structures. On the outside is the bark, which is itself divided into two layers, an outer layer called *cork* and an inner layer called *phloem*. The middle of the tree is the wood, or xylem. Between the wood of a tree and the inner bark, there is a thin band of living cells called the *cambium*, which is where two layers of new cells are formed as wood on the inside and as bark on the outside. In this way, as the tree grows older it increases in diameter.

More living cells grow at the ends of twigs and branches. Each year they extend farther, form leaves, and sometimes flowers in the growing season.

When a cross-section is cut through a tree, alternating bands of light and dark wood are found. The lighter bands are formed in the spring and have bigger cells, and the dark bands are formed in the autumn and consist of small, tightly packed cells. Scientists can match tree rings with large databases of similar trees and use these to determine the age of a tree.

FACT FILE

Trees are the largest living organisms on earth. The biggest tree, the Californian giant redwood, is over 300 ft. (100 m) high and has a trunk that is 35 ft. (11 m) thick. These ancient trees have very few branches and leaves, and are often scarred by forest fires and lightning strikes.

HOW DO LEAVES GROW?

Most green plants, including trees, have to manufacture their own food. They do this in their leaves (and in some plants the stems as well) through a process called *photosynthesis*.

The roots of a plant or tree take water from the soil by capillary action. The water eventually reaches the veins of the leaves. Carbon dioxide enters the tree's cells through the stomata in the leaves. When the sun is shining, cells in the leaves, called *chloroplasts*, which contain the green pigment chlorophyll, manufacture sugar, starches, and cellulose.

The sugar, starch, and cellulose are transported throughout the tree to where they are needed to produce new cells and add sweetness to the fruit.

Oxygen is a by-product of the process. It exits the tree through the stomata, together with most of the water that was absorbed by the roots.

FACT FILE

Energy from the sun evaporates water from the leaf surface through the stomata. This reduces pressure in the channels carrying water from the roots, so more water is drawn up the stem.

Water evaporates from the leaf surfaces into the surrounding air.

More water is taken up by the roots from the soil.

HOW DO FLOWERS DEVELOP THEIR SCENT?

Fragrant flowers contain substances called *essential oils* in their petals. There are thousands of different types and they are very complex. When these substances are broken down, or decomposed, the essential oils become volatile oils, which evaporate. When this happens, we can smell the fragrance the flower gives off. Some plants also have essential oils in other places. For example, citrus fruits contain essential oils in the pith of their fruits and give off strong scents if scratched. Others contain scents in their nuts, bark, or roots, such as ginger.

A flower's scent depends on the different chemicals in the volatile oils. Various combinations produce different fragrances.

The Arabians were the first to distil rose petals with water to produce rose water over 1,200 years ago. We still extract perfume from various flowers today.

FACT FILE

The hummingbird is the world's smallest bird. It can hover backwards as it feeds on flower nectar.

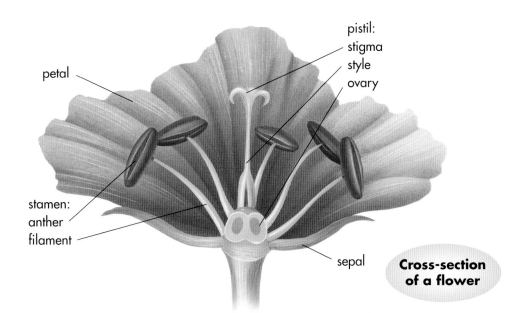

petal

pistil:
stigma
style
ovary

stamen:
anther
filament

sepal

Cross-section of a flower

WHAT HAPPENS IN FLOWERS?

Flowers come in many different shapes and sizes. Most contain the same four main parts, although these may not look the same in different flowers. In a "normal" flower, the sepals make up a green outer cup. Within the sepals are the petals, which are often colored. In the middle of the flower are one or more pistils, which form the female part of the flower. The bottom of this area is enlarged to form the ovary, which contains little round ovules that will later form into seeds if they are fertilized by the contents of a pollen grain from another flower. Pollen is produced by the stamen, the male organ of the flower. To fuse with an egg cell, a grain must land on the stigma and develop into a tube to reach the ovules at the bottom of the pistil. Pollen can be carried by wind or by insects feeding on nectar and moving from plant to plant.

FACT FILE

Pollen is the plant's equivalent of an animal's sperm. It carries the male reproductive genes. Pollen grains have a pattern, allowing the plant to be identified.

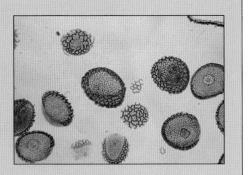

WHY DO PINE TREES STAY GREEN ALL YEAR?

In most trees, leaves give off enormous amounts of water. In some, more than 90 percent of the water absorbed by the roots and transported to the leaves is lost through evaporation. For most broad-leaved trees, such as oak, chestnuts, ash, and maples, this would be impossible to sustain in winter, when the ground is frozen. These deciduous trees drop their leaves in autumn to protect themselves. Certain trees, however, like pines and firs, have developed another strategy to avoid drying out. Their leaves are needle-like and covered in a waxy layer that prevents evaporation. They do not need to drop their leaves in autumn because they require very little water. When individual leaves do fall, new ones replace them so the branches never look bare.

Corsican pine

Norway spruce

FACT FILE

Fertilizers are used to make crops grow larger and faster. Crops are also regularly sprayed with pesticides and herbicides. Research indicates that the chemicals could cause health problems.

WHAT ARE PERENNIAL PLANTS?

Perennial plants survive from one year to the next. They usually grow quite slowly, and can afford to build up their strength before they need to produce seeds. The parts of perennial plants that are above the ground are generally killed by frost in the autumn. The roots and/or underground parts, though, live through the winter. Growth is renewed, and the cycle begins anew in the spring.

Perennial plants that grow in arid or desert conditions commonly survive dry times by becoming physiologically inactive. In some cases, they remain alive but are dehydrated until water becomes available. At this time, they rapidly absorb moisture through above-ground parts, swelling and resuming physiological activity. Some plants can absorb dew, which for many is the main water source. Mosses and lichens adopt this strategy, as do some flowering plants, which are sometimes called *resurrection plants*.

Daffodil

FACT FILE

In addition to looking like small bees, the flowers of bee orchids actually produce a female bee "smell." Therefore, they are highly attractive to male bees.

THE PREHISTORIC
WORLD

CONTENTS

HOW ARE PREHISTORIC TIMES CATEGORIZED? 102
WHAT HAVE WE LEARNED FROM PREHISTORY? 103

HOW ARE FOSSILS FORMED? 104
HOW ARE FOSSILS FOUND? 105

HOW DID LIFE BEGIN ON LAND? 106
WHY DID SOME FISH BECOME LAND-DWELLERS? 107

HOW DO WE KNOW WHAT DINOSAURS WERE LIKE? 108
HOW DID DINOSAURS EVOLVE? 109

WERE DINOSAURS SIMILAR TO MAMMALS? 110
HOW CLEVER WERE DINOSAURS? 111

HOW MANY DIFFERENT TYPES OF DINOSAUR WERE THERE? 112
HOW BIG WERE DINOSAURS? 113

DID DINOSAURS COMMUNICATE WITH EACH OTHER? 114
HOW COULD SMALL DINOSAURS ATTACK LARGER ONES? 115

HOW DID CARNIVOROUS DINOSAURS CATCH THEIR PREY? 116
HOW DID PLANT-EATING DINOSAURS FIND FOOD? 117

DID DINOSAURS LOOK AFTER THEIR YOUNG? 118
HOW BIG WERE DINOSAUR EGGS? 119

HOW DID DINOSAURS PROTECT THEMSELVES? 120
HOW DID DINOSAURS USE THEIR ARMOR? 121

WHEN DID FISH EVOLVE? 122
WHAT DID MARINE REPTILES LOOK LIKE? 123

WHAT SIZE WERE PTEROSAURS? 124
HOW DID PTEROSAURS FLY? 125

HOW DID PTEROSAURS MOVE ON THE GROUND? 126
WERE PTEROSAURS SIMILAR TO BIRDS OF TODAY? 127

WHY DID THE DINOSAURS DIE OUT? 128
DID CLIMATE AFFECT THE DINOSAURS' SURVIVAL? 129

HOW DID MAMMALS EVOLVE? 130
ARE MARSUPIALS SIMILAR TO THE FIRST MAMMALS? 131

HOW ARE PREHISTORIC TIMES CATEGORIZED?

Geological time covers many millions of years. It has been divided up into eras, which are periods of time identified by the fossilized forms of life from that period. The oldest era, called the Paleozoic, contains fossils ranging from many primitive life forms up to some of the earliest land-dwelling animals. During this era fish, amphibians, and early reptiles appeared.

The Mesozoic era was the age of giant reptiles, when dinosaurs ruled the world. The Cenozoic era, in which we still live, is the age of mammals and birds. All fossils can be placed in these eras, which are subdivided further into smaller periods as shown on the chart here.

FACT FILE

Now that the habits of dinosaurs are becoming better understood, museums are able to mount their fossilized remains in realistic poses that show how they lived.

Era	Period	
Cenozoic	Quaternary	
	Tertiary	65 -
Mesozoic	Cretaceous	145
	Jurassic	208 -
	Triassic	245 -
Paleozoic	Permian	290 -
	Carboniferous	362 -
	Devonian	408 -
	Silurian	439 -
	Ordovician	510 -
	Cambrian	570 -

WHAT HAVE WE LEARNED FROM PREHISTORY?

Almost everything that we know about life on earth before human beings evolved has been learned from fossils. Fossils are the remains of dead animals and plants that have been turned to stone over millions of years.

By studying these remains, scientists have been able to derive the type of animals that existed both on land and in water, and also the type of food they needed to live.

Records of prehistory and examples of fossils can be found in many of our modern museums.

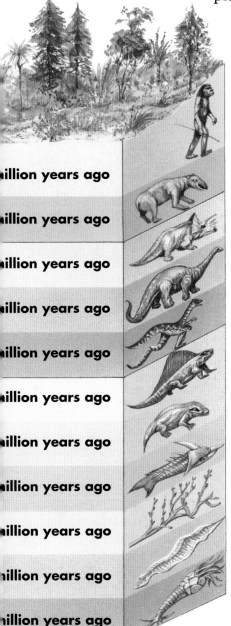

million years ago

million years ago

million years ago

million years ago

million years ago

million years ago

million years ago

million years ago

million years ago

million years ago

million years ago

FACT FILE

This particular shark, called *Carcharocles*, lived about 15 million years ago, and was about the size of a bus. Only its huge teeth have survived and so scientists were able to only estimate its actual size.

When an organism dies, the soft parts rot away.

The hard shell is covered with a layer of silt.

A hard mineral fossil is gradually formed.

HOW ARE FOSSILS FORMED?

Fossils result from the death of an animal that took place millions of years ago. The soft parts of the animal rot quickly, and the bones or shell are scattered by scavenging animals.

Some of these remains are buried in mud or sand. If they are not disturbed in any way, more mud is deposited until the remains are deeply buried. Under great pressure from deposits above, the mud eventually compacts into sedimentary rock.

Sometimes a fossil will retain the shape and structure of the hard parts of an animal, such as fossilized dinosaur bones. These are not the original bones because minerals have replaced them over the years, but they retain the same shape. Other fossils are just the impression of an animal or plant created when it was buried.

FACT FILE

Trilobites were once among the most abundant animals on earth. They lived only in the sea and survived for millions of years, evolving into some strangely shaped forms before suddenly becoming extinct.

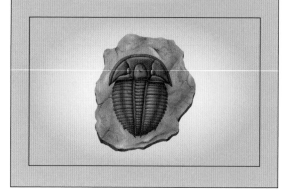

How are fossils found?

Every year, fossils are found that add to our knowledge of prehistoric life. Very often, they are discovered by ordinary people walking in rural areas. Places where soil is frequently being washed away from rocks, such as at the bottom of cliffs, are good places to look.

Fossils have been found accidentally by people working in mines or quarries. Sometimes they become exposed by erosion and can be seen sticking out of cliff faces.

Geologists are now able to identify those rock formations that are likely to contain fossils. More and more fossils are being found by well-organized expeditions.

Large numbers of new types of fossil are now being found in Mongolia and China. There, fossil hunters have unearthed what are probably the ancestors of modern birds. Paleontology is the scientific name for the study of fossils.

FACT FILE

This skeleton of the early reptile Dimetrodon is unusually complete. Most fossil remains consist only of fragments, which must be pieced together.

105

HOW DID LIFE BEGIN ON LAND?

Plants were the first living things on our planet, starting with very simple plants such as algae. Then mosses and liverworts developed, followed by ferns and other larger plants. Animals did not leave the sea to live on land until plants had become fully established, otherwise, there would have been no food for them.

Next were relatives of the spiders and scorpions which were probably the first creatures to leave the sea and actually colonize on land. Later, they evolved into larger and more complex forms of life. Amphibians multiplied rapidly, and the word actually means "living on land and in water."

FACT FILE

The first mammals lived alongside the dinosaurs. In comparison with reptiles they were tiny and insignificant like the Glyptodon below.

WHY DID SOME FISH BECOME LAND-DWELLERS?

Around 400 million years ago, fish began to creep out of the water onto land. The main reasons that an animal changes its habitat are to obtain fresh food supplies and to escape from its predators. Many fish were able to just wriggle along on land, but in order to lift their bodies clear off the ground ordinary fins were not strong enough. One of these fish is the coelacanth, a large fish up to 3 ft. (1 m) long with strange leglike fins. It was found to contain bones that were very like those of land-living vertebrate animals. Relatives of the coelacanth had leglike fins reinforced with bones, which allowed them to slither along like a modern crocodile.

Many ancient fish developed simple lungs which they used instead of their gills when they were out of the water.

FACT FILE

Baryonix is the only known fish-eating dinosaur, and uniquely it had huge claws on its front limbs.

HOW DO WE KNOW WHAT DINOSAURS WERE LIKE?

Although dinosaur remains are few, we can understand a great deal about them from their fossilized skeletons. We can calculate a dinosaur's weight by studying its bones. Heavy animals have massive bones to support their weight, while swift-moving hunters have very light, hollow bones. Muscles are firmly attached to bones, and although no trace of the muscles are left in the fossils, the points at which they attach can still be seen on the bones. These facts tell scientists how big the muscles must have been.

We know that a large digestive system is necessary to digest vegetable matter. The herbivores would have had massive barrel-shaped bodies, while carnivores would be thinner. The shape of the teeth tells scientists what type of food the dinosaurs ate.

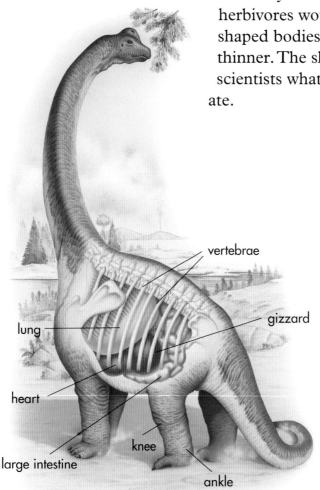

vertebrae

gizzard

lung

heart

large intestine

knee

ankle

FACT FILE

Much of what we know about dinosaurs is theory. Looking at the Carnotaurus, it had weak jaws and was not well equipped for hunting, so researchers theorized it fed on only small prey.

HOW DID DINOSAURS EVOLVE?

Dinosaurs were reptiles that evolved into the most varied kinds of any living creature. They ranged from tiny birdlike animals to monstrous beasts that were the largest animals to ever live on land.

The dinosaurs survived for about 150 million years. They were not all meat-eating killers as often portrayed in books and movies. Most dinosaurs were peaceful, browsing animals about the size of modern farm livestock.

The main thing that distinguishes dinosaurs from other reptiles was the way their body was supported by their legs. The legs of ancient and existing reptiles stuck out sideways, so the body dragged on the ground for most of the time. It was raised briefly when the animal ran. The skeletons of dinosaurs developed so the legs were beneath the body, raising the whole body off the ground.

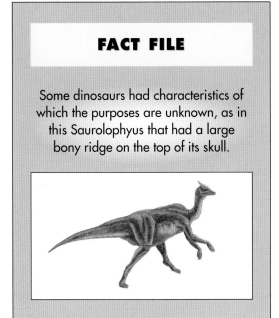

FACT FILE

Some dinosaurs had characteristics of which the purposes are unknown, as in this Saurolophyus that had a large bony ridge on the top of its skull.

WERE DINOSAURS SIMILAR TO MAMMALS?

Dimetrodon

As dinosaurs multiplied they became more diverse. Among them were mammal-like reptiles called *synapsids*. One of these, Dimetrodon, had a sail-like structure on its back. The sail may have helped to control the body temperature. By turning the sail to face the sun, these cold-blooded reptiles could absorb heat.

Other mammal-like reptiles, called *dicynodonts*, are thought to have become warm-blooded and gradually evolved into true mammals.

Another group of reptiles, called *archosaurs*, appeared during the Triassic period. Most of them were predators, and they gave rise to animals such as dinosaurs and crocodiles. The archosaurs were a group of animals in which the modification to the hips and legs developed. This led to the animal being able to support its own weight and to stand upright.

FACT FILE

Triceratops resembled the modern rhinoceros and probably lived a similar lifestyle. It was one of a large family of plant-eating dinosaurs that all had spiked skulls and a frill of bone covering their necks.

How intelligent were dinosaurs?

Troodon

It is difficult to assess the intelligence of an extinct animal. But we do know that the intelligence of dinosaurs must have been sufficient for their way of life: otherwise, they would not have survived for millions of years. Some of the plant-eating dinosaurs certainly had very small brains in proportion to their size. However, a large brain is not important in an animal that is too enormous to be attacked and has little to think about except eating. On the other hand, some of the predatory dinosaurs had quite large brains that allowed them to think quickly as they went after their prey.

The most intelligent dinosaur was probably the Troodon, which was only about the size of a large domestic dog. Its brain was very large in proportion to its size. It could run very fast, swerving and ducking to catch its prey. It had all the right physical attributes to have evolved into an intelligent form of life, but it became extinct with all the other dinosaurs.

FACT FILE

In comparison with their size, the brain of the smallest dinosaur predators were the biggest. This enabled them to think, react, and move quicker.

HOW MANY DIFFERENT TYPES OF DINOSAUR WERE THERE?

Pachycephalosaurus

There were thousands of different species of dinosaur, and we have discovered only a small number of them. It is important to understand how rare fossils are. There were a few dinosaur species that must have been very common, like Iguanodon, which left many fossils. Others were probably scarce when they were alive, or they lived in regions where fossilization was unlikely, so there are few remains of those dinosaurs.

Herbivores often lived in groups or herds, but carnivores were usually more solitary and so their fossils are more rare. Many of the better-known dinosaurs are known from a single fossil, or one or two bones, and scientists must calculate the shape and size from these clues.

FACT FILE

Although in many ways the Ouranosaurus was a typical plant-eating dinosaur, it had a remarkable sail-like crest on its back and tail. Its function is not known.

HOW BIG WERE DINOSAURS?

Euoplocephalus

Dinosaurs varied considerably in size. Some were only about the size of a chicken, or even smaller. Compsognathus was only about 28 inches (70 cm) long and slightly built. It was an agile and fast-moving creature and is thought to have lived on insects and small animals. The skeleton of this dinosaur is very similar to that of a modern bird.

Scientists cannot agree on the maximum size of giant dinosaurs. It is thought that Brachiosaurus was the largest, and is thought to have been about 100 ft. (30 m) long and to have weighed as much as 128 tons (130 tonnes). This would make it by far the heaviest land animal to have ever existed. The Sauroposeidon has been described as being as high as 56 ft. (17.2 m), making it three times the height of the tallest giraffe.

FACT FILE

The biggest mammal to have lived on the earth actually preceded dinosaurs. It was called the *Indicotherium* and was big enough to push over trees which were too tall for it to graze upon.

113

DID DINOSAURS COMMUNICATE WITH EACH OTHER?

There is strong evidence that some plant-eating dinosaurs could make a lot of noise, although we do not know this for sure.

Many duck-billed dinosaurs had a large, bony structure on their head, which was probably used to amplify sound, much like the body of a guitar. Hollow air passages in the bony structure allowed the dinosaur to produce booming cries.

In some species, the shape of the crest and the sounds produced varied between individual animals, helping herd members to locate each other. Males probably had their own sounds they used in their mating displays. The unusual crest on the Parasaurolophus appears to have acted as an echo chamber, allowing this dinosaur to have a very loud, booming cry.

FACT FILE

It is believed that the plates on the back of some dinosaurs were used to frighten rival animals. The sharp spikes along the edge of the body of Sauropelta would have stopped any predator from getting at its soft underbelly.

Parasaurolophus

HOW COULD SMALL DINOSAURS ATTACK LARGER ONES?

Deinonychus

Standing about as tall as a man, Deinonychus was a fast-moving and intelligent predator that grasped its prey with clawed front limbs before ripping them apart with the huge claw on its hind foot.

Some of the smaller dinosaurs may have hunted in packs, like modern wolves. By working together, they would have been able to kill much larger animals.

The Deinonychus was lightly built so it could run extremely fast. This hunter had a stiff tail which it probably used to steer itself and change direction quickly while chasing its prey. It also had very sharp teeth and powerful arms with grasping claws. The most unusual feature was a large upturned claw on its foot which could be swiveled downwards to slash its prey with its muscular hind legs. This would probably have caused its prey to bleed to death.

FACT FILE

Many dinosaurs avoided attack in the best way they could. This Velociraptor was small but heavily armed with a ripping claw on its hand leg. It probably hunted in packs.

HOW DID CARNIVOROUS DINOSAURS CATCH THEIR PREY?

All meat-eating dinosaurs were about the same shape, but they varied in size. They all belonged to a group called *theropods*, meaning "beast feet."

The giant dinosaurs like Tyrannosaurus rex probably ambushed their prey, charging at them with their jaws wide open. They could run at a speed of 32 mph (50 kph), although probably for only a short distance. The impact of eight tons (seven tonnes) of dinosaur hitting its prey with a jagged mouthful of teeth would most likely kill most animals.

Many smaller dinosaurs had powerful front limbs and claws, and could cling to their prey while biting it.

FACT FILE

Plant-eating dinosaurs had long necks to enable them to reach trees, which were their main source of food.

Saltasaurus

Tyrannosaurus rex, usually just called T-rex, was the largest and most fearsome land-living predator ever to have lived.

Tyrannosaurus rex

HOW DID PLANT-EATING DINOSAURS FIND FOOD?

Hadrosaurus

Hadrosaurus was a large plant-eater that walked sometimes on two legs and other times on four.

The type of food that plant-eating dinosaurs fed on depended on their type of mouth. Some had broad mouths like a duck's bill and those probably grazed on a mixture of plants. Dinosaurs with narrow jaws, most likely selected particular plants to eat.

The long-necked sauropods probably grazed on leaves and shoots. Large herds of sauropods would have caused tremendous destruction by feeding in this manner and may have used their great weight to push trees over so they would be easier to reach.

A herd of sauropods would have cleared a large area of trees, creating large spaces of open ground where smaller dinosaurs could graze. Dinosaurs with cutting beaks would keep vegetation short.

FACT FILE

The diets of some dinosaurs are a complete mystery. For example, the Segnosaurus could have eaten termites, fish, or plants.

DID DINOSAURS LOOK AFTER THEIR YOUNG?

Large numbers of Protoceratops remains have been found in the Gobi desert, including eggs and young. These animals seem to have nested in large groups and probably cared for their young.

It was thought at one time that dinosaurs laid their eggs in isolated places. But in 1978, a remarkable find was made in the state of Montana. Fifteen Maiasaurus babies were found scattered around a large mound-shaped structure, together with many broken eggshells. The babies were not just hatched because their teeth were partly worn away. The nest itself was about 7 ft. (2 m) across and covered with vegetation.

FACT FILE

The eggs of Orodromeus have been found broken open from the inside as the young hatched out. The baby dinosaurs are thought to have foraged for their food while being guarded by adults.

In the Gobi desert, the pig-sized dinosaur Protoceratops dug holes in the sand and buried her eggs. She left them to hatch in the heat of the sand while she guarded them from predators. The eggs were arranged in careful circles, in layers. It is thought the mother dinosaur positioned herself above the nest as she laid each egg.

HOW BIG WERE DINOSAUR EGGS?

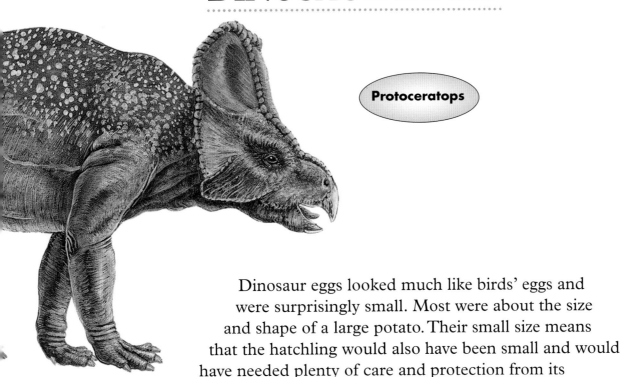

Protoceratops

Dinosaur eggs looked much like birds' eggs and were surprisingly small. Most were about the size and shape of a large potato. Their small size means that the hatchling would also have been small and would have needed plenty of care and protection from its parents.

When Orodromeus nests were discovered, other dinosaur eggs were found between them. These eggs were smaller and were laid in straight lines. It has recently been found that they are the eggs of a small predator, called the *Troodon*. It appears to have laid its eggs in the Orodromeus colony to get protection from other predators. This habit is similar to that of modern cuckoos and their relatives, although they also use another species of bird to raise their young.

FACT FILE

The Oviraptor was an odd dinosaur that may have lived entirely on the eggs of other dinosaurs. It was bird-shaped, with a powerful beak for crushing eggs and did not have any teeth.

Euoplocephalus

HOW DID DINOSAURS PROTECT THEMSELVES?

Dinosaurs had various ways of protecting themselves. First, they might just have been too big to be defeated and eaten. Some dinosaurs could run very fast, which means they could escape their predators. Finally, a slow-moving dinosaur may have been covered with spikes and horns to help deter attackers.

FACT FILE

Although the sides of its body were less heavily armored than many of its relatives, the underside of the Minmi was well-protected by its covering of tough, bony plates.

120

In addition to being covered with jointed armor and defensive spines, the Euoplocephalus carried a massive club on the end of its tail which would have crushed any predator.

HOW DID DINOSAURS USE THEIR ARMOR?

FACT FILE

Although some dinosaurs could not run very fast at all, they had other ways of defending themselves. The Shunasaurus had a club on its tail that it would wield in defense.

There are several theories about why some dinosaurs had armor on parts of their bodies. The plates on the back of the Stegosaurus could have been used to frighten rival animals or to help regulate body temperature. It has even been suggested that the plates could have folded flat to make a sheet of armor over the animal's back. The whole head of an Ankylosaur was covered with protective plates, which even extended over the eyes. Others used their tails for defense.

WHEN DID FISH EVOLVE?

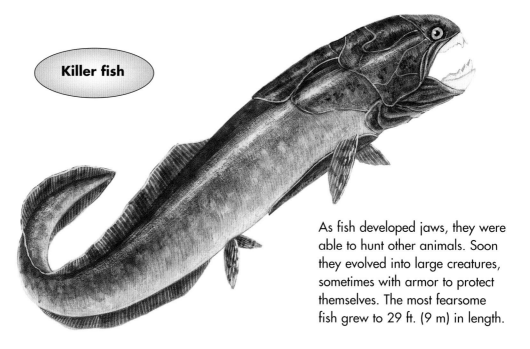

Killer fish

As fish developed jaws, they were able to hunt other animals. Soon they evolved into large creatures, sometimes with armor to protect themselves. The most fearsome fish grew to 29 ft. (9 m) in length.

Fossils show that the first fish originated in the Ordovician Period, which began about 460,000,000 years ago. These fish were jawless and the most primitive. Their mouths had a simple opening, suited to feeding on the tiny animals that lay hidden in the mud.

Next came fish with jaws. Jaws permitted fish to explore various food sources and to feed more efficiently. Early fish with jaws are called *placoderms*. The jaws evolved from a set of gill arches that were present in the jawless fish. Gill arches are the bony supports of the gills.

From these placoderms came our present-day fish, the sharks and bony fish.

FACT FILE

Ammonites were relatives of the modern octopus and squid. They secreted a hard shell and lived in a small compartment. A new compartment was added as they grew, eventually producing a spiral shell.

WHAT DID MARINE REPTILES LOOK LIKE?

The Ichthyosaurs looked much like modern dolphins but were totally aquatic reptiles that gave birth to live young.

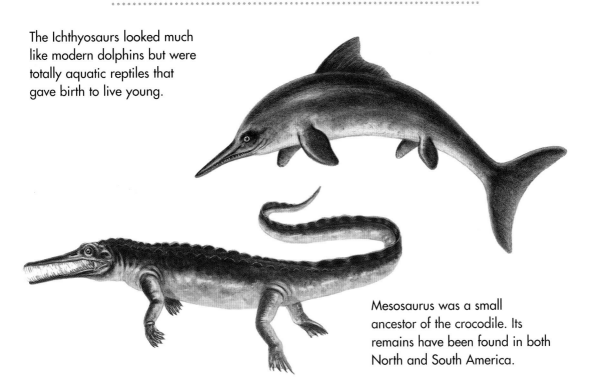

Mesosaurus was a small ancestor of the crocodile. Its remains have been found in both North and South America.

Many reptiles returned to the sea. Some of the most familiar ones are the Plesiosaurs, large animals with barrel-like bodies and long snaky necks. They did not have a flexible body. They rowed themselves along by waving their fin-like front and rear limbs up and down.

Pliosaurs were relatives of the Plesiosaurs but had shorter necks and massive skulls armed with enormous teeth. They were the largest and most powerful predators ever known.

Turtles also developed at about the same time. Early turtles did not have complete shells.

FACT FILE

Although you might think a crocodile is a dinosaur, you would be wrong. Although they both evolved from the same type of ancestors, crocodiles have changed very little over millions of years.

WHAT SIZE WERE PTEROSAURS?

Several reptiles developed the ability to glide, but the pterosaurs were the only ones to develop true flight. Their arms were quite short and their wings were supported by an enormously long fourth finger, leaving the other fingers free to function as a hand. A thin, skin-like membrane was stretched from its elongated finger to the sides of the body and sometimes to the hind legs.

The whole body was extremely light, with hollow bones. Many pterosaurs lived a similar life to the modern seagull and albatross. One pterosaur discovered, the Quetzalcoatlus, had a wing span more than 48 ft. (15 m), which is larger than that of many light planes.

FACT FILE

The Pterodactylus was a very small flying reptile, smaller than a modern pigeon and much lighter in build. It had a wing span of 15 in. (40 cm) across, which means it would have been a fast and agile flyer.

Scientists were astounded when the remains of Quetzalcoatlus were found. It proved to be the largest flying creature to have ever existed.

How did pterosaurs fly?

Rhamporhyncus was a moderate-sized pterosaur with a 5½ ft. (1.75 m) wing span. Its long tail was tipped with an unusual diamond-shaped piece of skin that may have helped stabilize it in flight.

It was once believed that the pterosaurs were unable to flap their wings and fly like a bird. They probably launched themselves off cliffs and glided on upward currents of air.

More recently, however, it has been suggested that pterosaurs were actually very efficient flyers. Some of the smallest types would not have been very effective gliders and must have fluttered their wings like modern birds. This would not have been possible for the giant pterosaurs, which must have been true gliders.

Pterosaurs did not have feathers, because their large wings were more like those of a bat than a bird. However, pterosaurs did have fur. This suggests that they were probably warm-blooded.

FACT FILE

The small predatory therapod dinosaur Campsognathus resembles Archaeopteryx so closely that the remains of the two animals have often been confused. This seems to prove the dinosaur ancestry to birds.

Pteranodon was a large and efficient flyer. It had a huge backward-pointing crest on its head, which may have been used as a rudder during gliding flight.

HOW DID PTEROSAURS MOVE ON THE GROUND?

Scientists are not really sure how pterosaurs moved about on the ground. We know that their huge wings could not be folded away as neatly as those of a modern bird, and they would have been very awkward on the ground.

Most paleontologists think that pterosaurs probably scuttled around on their hands and on the feet of their hind legs, with their wings folded and trailing behind them.

Another view is that some pterosaurs may have scuttled about upright, running on their hind legs. Some people think that they may have been scavengers like vultures, but it is hard to imagine this because of their size and awkwardness.

FACT FILE

Some of the giant birds, like the Diatryma, were unable to fly. They were important predators and could tackle almost any prey with their massive beaks.

WERE PTEROSAURS SIMILAR TO BIRDS OF TODAY?

Despite their apparent similarities, pterosaurs were quite different in structure to birds, and they never developed the powerful breast muscles needed to beat their wings in the same way as birds.

Also, they could not fold their wings away like modern birds, so they would always have been clumsy when moving on the ground.

Modern birds do not have teeth, and their tailbone is reduced to a small stump. Fossils of a whole range of feathered dinosaurs are now found in many countries and especially in China. All these creatures were built along the same lines as birds. Some were undoubtedly dinosaurs and would have used their feathered forelimbs to help them run, rather than fly.

FACT FILE

The ungainly and primitive Hoatzin lives in South America. Its young show their reptile ancestry by having claws on their wings that they use to climb about in trees.

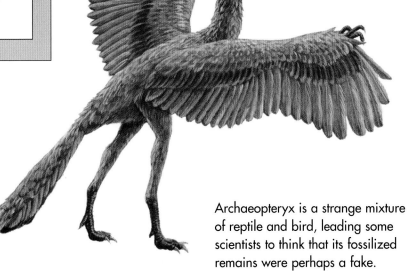

Archaeopteryx is a strange mixture of reptile and bird, leading some scientists to think that its fossilized remains were perhaps a fake.

FACT FILE

Huge meteorite craters still exist, though most became eroded after millions of years and are not as obvious as this crater in the state of Arizona.

WHY DID THE DINOSAURS DIE OUT?

Dinosaurs lived for a long time – some 150 million years – before they died out about 65 million years ago. During their time on the earth they dominated the land, while their reptile relatives dominated the sea and the air. Before the dinosaurs disappeared completely, there were two mass extinctions when a large number of species died out. The dinosaurs survived, however, until the end of the Cretaceous Period.

One theory is that dinosaurs became extinct as a result of climate change after a huge meteor or a small asteroid struck the earth.

The other theory is that it coincided with a period of high volcanic activity, which could have wiped out the whole population. However, it was not only the dinosaurs that became extinct. At the same time, most marine reptiles and pterosaurs also died out, as did tiny plankton whose shells form chalk deposits, ammonites, and the remaining species of trilobites. It is difficult to figure out the exact causes of this extinction, especially since some creatures, like sea turtles, survived.

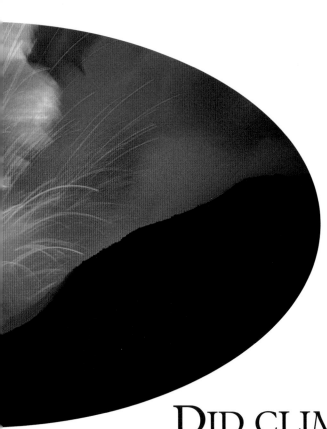

High volcanic activity could have contributed to the dinosaurs' extinction.

DID CLIMATE AFFECT THE DINOSAURS' SURVIVAL?

During the late Cretaceous Period, the world's continents were drifting into new positions. This constant shifting within the crust led to a huge increase in volcanic activity. Volcanoes spewed out hot lava and gases, which could have built up in the atmosphere to such high levels that they affected dinosaurs and their plant food.

Other climatic changes, like the Ice Age, may have wiped out many species of dinosaur that were unable to adapt to the extreme cold.

FACT FILE

The earth went through some incredible climate changes during the era of the dinosaurs, and one of the theories regarding their extinction would have been the Ice Age. There are very few plants or animals that could have survived this extreme cold.

HOW DID MAMMALS EVOLVE?

Thylacosmilus

A group of mammal-like reptiles preceded the appearance of the dinosaurs. These early mammals gradually disappeared, however, during the Triassic Period and were replaced by the true mammals.

It is hard to determine which of these extinct animals was a reptile and which was a mammal. It is quite probable that the later reptiles had hair and other mammal-like characteristics. The first mammals were small and were vulnerable to all the fierce dinosaur predators. Once the dinosaurs died out, the mammals were able to develop properly and evolve. Eventually, the mammals grew into forms that were almost as gigantic as their dinosaur predecessors.

Thylacosmilus was a typical example of the saber-tooth cats, with long canine teeth that were used to stab its prey.

FACT FILE

Mammoths closely resembled modern elephants but were covered with thick, coarse hair and were adapted to live in the cold tundra regions. They survived in northern Arctic regions until well after the appearance of human beings, who hunted them until they were extinct.

ARE MARSUPIALS SIMILAR TO THE FIRST MAMMALS?

Researchers think that marsupials, like the kangaroo, are actually primitive mammals because they give birth to tiny, underdeveloped young. The young are raised in a pouch until they are developed enough to live on their own. There are two kinds of mammals, however, that still lay eggs like their reptile ancestors. Both the duck-billed platypus and the spiny anteater, or *echidna*, live in Australia. They lay eggs and the hatchlings are placed in a pouch on their mother's stomach. Unlike reptiles' young, these babies are nourished by their mother's milk. These two very unusual animals give us some indication about how the earliest mammals may have developed.

FACT FILE

Also known as Zeuglodon, Basilosaurus is the most commonly found of the ancient fossil whales. It was a predator like modern dolphins. When whales die, their remains usually sink in deep water where they are unlikely to form fossils.

EARTH AND SPACE

CONTENTS

WHAT IS A DAY? 134
WHAT IS A HEMISPHERE? 135

HOW DEEP IS THE PACIFIC OCEAN? 136
WHAT CAUSES TIDES? 137

WHAT ARE OCEAN TRENCHES? 138
WHAT ARE CURRENTS? 139

HOW DID THE CONTINENTS USED TO LOOK? 140
WHAT IS PLATE TECTONICS? 141

WHAT GIVES THE SEA-FLOOR ITS SHAPE? 142
WHAT IS THE CONTINENTAL SHELF? 143

WHY DOES LAND EROSION OCCUR? 144
WHAT ERODES THE DESERTS? 145

WHY DO GLACIERS FORM? 146
WHAT IS AN ICE SHEET? 147

WHAT GIVES A RIVER ITS SHAPE? 148
WHAT GIVES A COASTLINE ITS SHAPE? 149

WHAT IS CLIMATE? 150
WHAT IS A SAVANNA? 151

WHAT IS PRECIPITATION? 152
WHY DOES FLOODING OCCUR? 153

WHAT ARE THE MOST EXTREME TEMPERATURES EVER RECORDED? 154
WHEN DO DROUGHTS OCCUR? 155

WHAT IS SALINE WATER? 156
WHAT IS IRRIGATION? 157

WHAT IS THE WATER CYCLE? 158
WHAT IS THE WATER TABLE? 159

WHAT IS A TSUNAMI? 160
WHAT IS AN EYEWALL? 161

WHAT IS ACID RAIN? 162
WHY DOES DEFORESTATION OCCUR? 163

HOW BIG ARE ASTEROIDS? 164
HOW ARE METEORITES FORMED? 165

WHAT IS A FALLING STAR? 166
HOW DO STARS MAKE PICTURES? 167

HOW MUCH DOES THE ATMOSPHERE WEIGH? 168
HOW OLD IS THE EARTH? 169

WHY DON'T PLANETS COLLIDE? 170
HOW WAS THE LIGHT-YEAR DISCOVERED? 171

HOW FAR DOES OUTER SPACE GO? 172
HOW FAST DOES THE EARTH MOVE? 173

HOW BIG IS THE UNIVERSE? 174
WHAT IS THE EARTH MADE OF? 175

HOW ARE STARS FORMED? 176
HOW FAR AWAY ARE THE STARS? 177

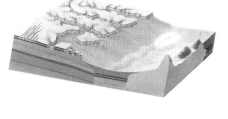

Alice Springs: Desert

°F
104
86
50
32
inches
16
12
8
4
0

Jan. May Aug. Dec.

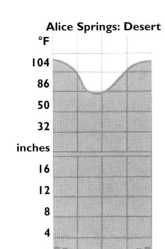

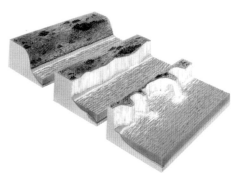

WHAT IS A DAY?

For early peoples, the only changes that were truly regular were the motions of objects in the sky. The most obvious of these changes was the alternating daylight and darkness caused by the rising and setting of the sun. Each of these cycles of the sun came to be called a *day*. Another regular change in the sky was the change in the visible shape of the moon. Each cycle of the moon takes about 29½ days, or a month. The cycle of the seasons gave people an even longer unit of time.

There is no regular change in the sky that lasts seven days, to represent the week. The seven-day week came from the Jewish custom of observing a Sabbath (day of rest) every seventh day. The division of a day into 24 hours, an hour into 60 minutes, and a minute into 60 seconds probably came from the ancient Babylonians.

FACT FILE

Some clock faces are divided into 24 hours. On such a clock, 9 A.M. would be shown as 0900 and 4 P.M. would be 1600. This system avoids confusion between the morning and evening hours.

JUNE 21   North Pole: 24 hours daylight

N

13.5 hours dayl.

0° SUN'S RA

12 hours dayli

10.5 hours daylig

S

South Pole: 24 hours darkness

WHAT IS A HEMISPHERE?

FACT FILE

The equator is an imaginary line drawn around the outside of the earth. It divides the earth into two halves, called *hemispheres*. The equator was invented by mapmakers because it makes a convenient point from which to measure distances north and south.

Tropic of Cancer

Equator

Tropic of Capricorn

A hemisphere is the name given to any half of any globe, including the earth. It is derived from the Greek for "half a sphere."

For convenience, geographers divide the earth into hemispheres with the equator as a boundary. Everything north of the equator is in the northern hemisphere, while everything to south lies in the southern hemisphere. The equator lies at an equal distance from the geographic North and South Poles.

Because land is not distributed evenly across the surface of the earth, the globe may also be divided into land and water hemispheres, the former centered near London and the latter near New Zealand.

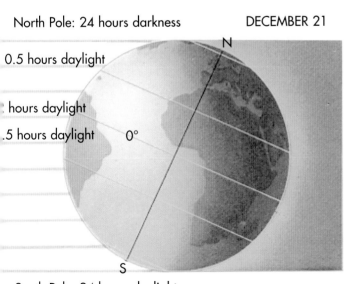

North Pole: 24 hours darkness   DECEMBER 21

0.5 hours daylight

hours daylight

.5 hours daylight   0°

South Pole: 24 hours daylight

HOW DEEP IS THE PACIFIC OCEAN?

The Pacific Ocean, the largest and deepest of the world's four oceans, covers more than a third of the earth's surface and contains more than half of its free water. The floor of the Pacific Ocean, which has an average depth of around 14,000 ft. (4,300 m), is mainly a deep-sea plain. The name *Pacific*, which means "peaceful," was given to it by the Portuguese navigator Ferdinand Magellan in 1520. The Pacific is the oldest of the existing ocean basins, its oldest rocks having been dated at 200 million years.

The Pacific Ocean is bordered on the east by the North and South American continents; on the north by the Bering Strait; on the west by Asia, the Malay Archipelago, and Australia; and on the south by Antarctica.

223 sq. mi. of the earth's surface is covered by water

FACT FILE

The Pacific Ocean contains more than 30,000 islands. Their total land area, however, amounts to only one-quarter of one percent of the ocean's surface area.

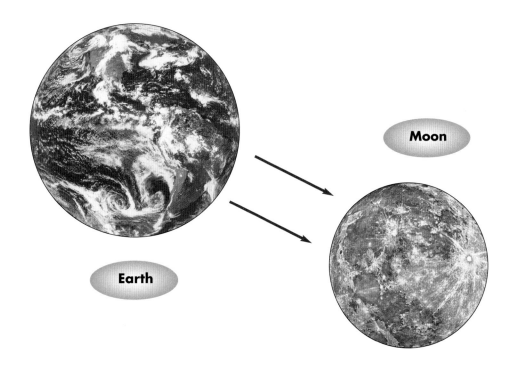

Moon

Earth

WHAT CAUSES TIDES?

The daily rise and fall of the ocean's tides occur because of the moon's pull of gravity. As the earth spins round, the water in the oceans is "pulled" towards the moon slightly, making a bulge. There is a corresponding bulge on the other side of the earth. Wherever the bulges are positioned, it is high tide. In between, the water is shallower and so it is low tide. High tides occur every 25 hours, because at the same time that the earth is spinning on its axis, the moon is traveling around the earth once every 27½ days. This means that high tides are about one hour later every day.

FACT FILE

Spring tides are tides with unusually high ranges twice each month when the sun, earth, and moon are in line. They can be especially high in the spring and autumn.

WHAT ARE OCEAN TRENCHES?

FACT FILE

For centuries, most people assumed that the cold, black depths of the ocean supported little or no life. Scientists have since discovered a great variety of living things in the deep sea.

Trenches are the deepest parts of the ocean. Many trenches occur in the Pacific Ocean, especially in its western portion. Most trenches are long, narrow, and deep, 2 to 2.5 miles (3 to 4 km) below the surrounding sea floor. The greatest depth anywhere in the ocean is found in the Mariana Trench, southeast of Japan. It plunges more than 6.8 miles (11 km) below sea level. Frequent earthquakes and volcanic eruptions occur along the trenches because this is where oceanic crust is forced underneath the continental crust.

Deep-sea fish are very different from those found in shallow waters

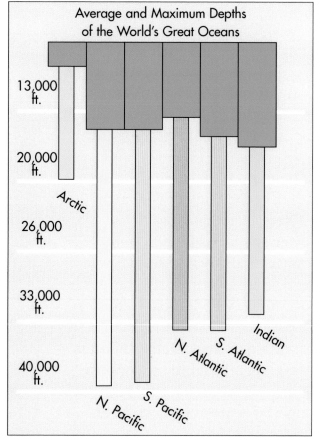

Average and Maximum Depths of the World's Great Oceans

13,000 ft.

20,000 ft.

Arctic

26,000 ft.

33,000 ft.

N. Atlantic   S. Atlantic   Indian

40,000 ft.

N. Pacific   S. Pacific

WHAT ARE CURRENTS?

The oceans are moved by the wind on their surface and from the movement inside the ocean. Ocean currents can move a large amount of heat around the earth and can control the climate. The way the water circulates depends on the spinning of the earth. The water in the northern hemisphere spins clockwise, and the water in the southern hemisphere spins counter-clockwise. The ocean currents are different in summer and winter. The wind direction can change which ocean current will influence the weather in a given country. A cold ocean current can make the weather cold, while a warm ocean current can make the weather warm.

FACT FILE

A whirlpool is a mass of water which spins around and around rapidly, with great force. It may occur when opposing currents meet, or it may be caused by wind.

Ocean currents

Summer in Northern Hemisphere

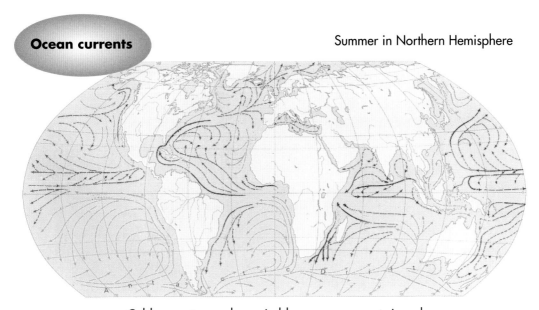

Cold currents are shown in blue, warm currents in red

200 million years ago

135 million years ago

Present day

150 million years' time

HOW DID THE CONTINENTS USED TO LOOK?

When the earth formed, the lighter elements floated to the surface where they cooled to form a crust. Although the first rocks were formed over 3,500 years ago, they have not stayed the same. They have been changed from forces on the inside and the outside of the earth. The coastlines on each side of the Atlantic appear to fit like a jigsaw puzzle. Researchers believe that all the land masses were once joined together forming a super continent called *Pangaea*.
This split up to form the continents we know today.

FACT FILE

Movement of land is still taking place as India and Asia collide, forming the Himalayas. This is called *continental drift*.

WHAT IS PLATE TECTONICS?

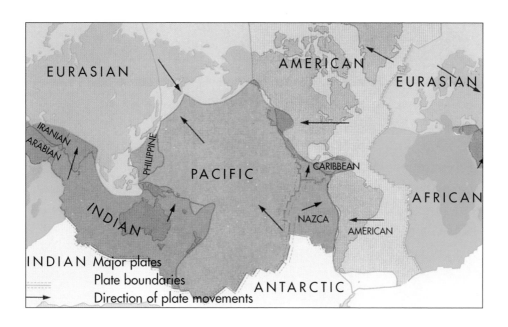

INDIAN Major plates
Plate boundaries
Direction of plate movements

Plate tectonics theory explains the major features of the earth's surface, both on land and under the oceans – how mountains are formed, what is happening in deep-sea trenches, and why earthquakes and volcanoes occur where they do. The earth's crust is broken into fragments, called *plates*. These vary in size and move in response to currents in the slowly flowing but solid mantle rock beneath. The plates move at different speeds, ranging from ½ to 4 inches (1 to 10 cm) a year. Scientists make these measurements by bouncing lasers from various points on the earth off reflectors left on the moon by Apollo astronauts, and calculate the relative difference and direction of motion.

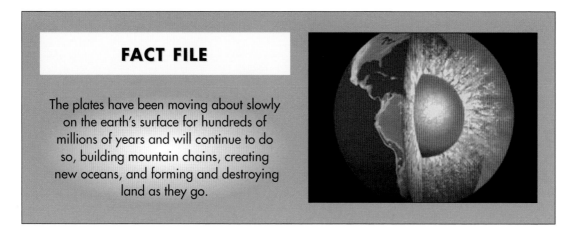

FACT FILE

The plates have been moving about slowly on the earth's surface for hundreds of millions of years and will continue to do so, building mountain chains, creating new oceans, and forming and destroying land as they go.

WHAT GIVES THE SEA-FLOOR ITS SHAPE?

The bottom of the ocean has features as varied as those on land. Huge plains spread out across the ocean floor, and long mountain chains rise toward the surface. Volcanoes erupt from the ocean bottom, and deep valleys cut through the floor. In the early 1960s, a theory called *sea-floor spreading* provided an explanation. According to the theory, the circulating currents deep within the mantle pull the sea-floor apart, carrying the continents with it. Molten magma is forced by pressure up into central valleys of the mid-ocean ridges. The magma cools and hardens to form new sea-floor and pushes older floor away. At the edges of the plate, some of the old oceanic crust dives under the continents.

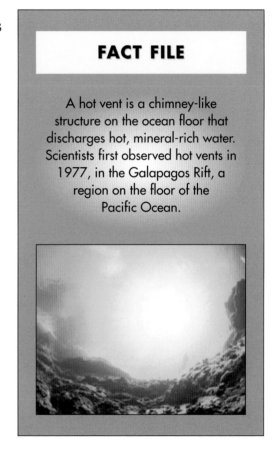

FACT FILE

A hot vent is a chimney-like structure on the ocean floor that discharges hot, mineral-rich water. Scientists first observed hot vents in 1977, in the Galapagos Rift, a region on the floor of the Pacific Ocean.

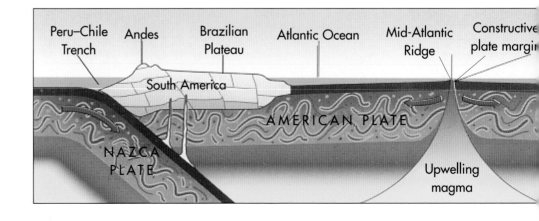

Peru–Chile Trench · Andes · Brazilian Plateau · Atlantic Ocean · Mid-Atlantic Ridge · Constructive plate margin · South America · AMERICAN PLATE · NAZCA PLATE · Upwelling magma

WHAT IS THE CONTINENTAL SHELF?

FACT FILE

The continental rise consists of sediment from the continental shelf that accumulates at the bottom of the slope. These deposits can extend up to 600 miles (1,000 km) from the slope.

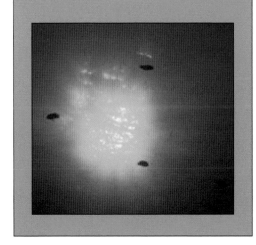

The continental margin is the area that separates the part of a continent above sea level from the deep sea floor. It consists of three parts, the continental shelf, the continental slope, and the continental rise.

The continental shelf begins at the shoreline and slopes gently underwater to an average depth of about 440 ft. (135 m). The width of the continental shelf averages 47 miles (75 km), although in some places it is thousands of miles across and in others only a few feet. Valleys of varying depths cut through the shelf. At the edge of the continental shelf, there is an abrupt change in steepness, and the continental slope plunges down to the continental rise or, in some cases, to ocean trenches.

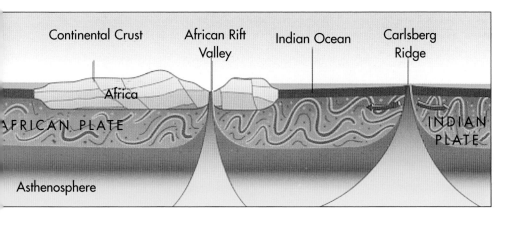

Continental Crust African Rift Valley Indian Ocean Carlsberg Ridge

Africa

AFRICAN PLATE INDIAN PLATE

Asthenosphere

WHY DOES LAND EROSION OCCUR?

Erosion is a process through which rock and soil are broken loose from the earth's surface in one place and moved elsewhere. Natural erosion alters the shape of the land by wearing down mountains and filling in valleys and rivers with sediment. It is usually a slow process that makes little difference in thousands of years.

Erosion begins with weathering, by the action of rain and snow, rivers, wind, and ice, including glaciers. Sediments are eventually carried down from the mountains to the plains below, creating fertile land. If soil is left bare, rain and wind will wash it into streams and rivers, and it will eventually be washed out to sea and end up on the ocean floor.

FACT FILE

Erosion can be sped up by activities such as farming and forestry. Landslides are one catastrophic result when too much supporting vegetation is lost.

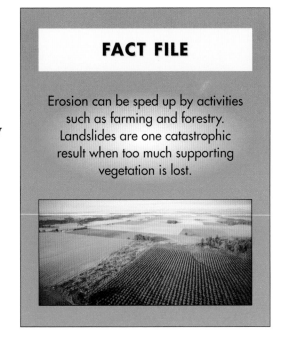

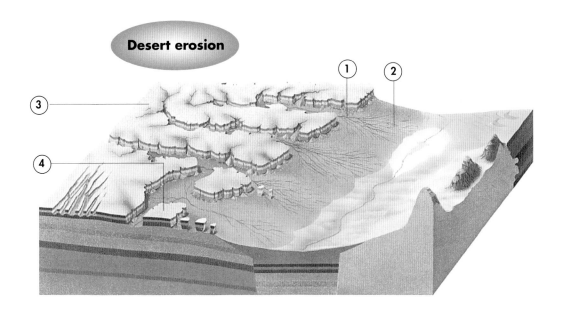

Desert erosion

WHAT ERODES THE DESERTS?

A dry desert landscape includes surface features that have been created over thousands of years by erosion of wind and the resulting deposit of silt and sand. After a rain, water fills the usually dry stream channels called *wadis* ①. The rapidly flowing water cuts into the soft rocks of desert mountains and carries sediments down through canyons and deposits sediments in fan-shaped forms known as *alluvial fans* ②.

Sometimes, the streams carry large amounts of water out into low areas in the desert plains that form temporary lakes. The water that collects in these lakes either evaporates or seeps into the ground. Water erosion in deserts also creates big, flat-topped hills known as *mesas* ③ and smaller flat-topped hills called *buttes* ④.

Sand dunes are not fixed features but move with the prevailing wind.

WHY DO GLACIERS FORM?

Glacier

Debris carried
by glacier

Deposited debris

Glaciers begin to form on mountains when the winter snowfall outweighs the summer snowmelt and evaporation. The excess snow builds up in layers over years. The increasing weight of successive layers of snow compresses the crystals below the surface, eventually turning them into dense, blue glacial ice. The glacier becomes so massive that it moves down the mountain slope under the force of gravity, gouging out rock from the sides and floor of the valley. The top of the glacier continues to be fed with fresh snow.

FACT FILE

Glaciers have shaped most of the world's highest mountains, carving out huge valleys. Lakes in mountain regions are formed from flooded glacial valleys that become dammed by debris as the glacier melts.

WHAT IS AN ICE SHEET?

Over 10,000 years ago, about a third of the land surface was covered with ice. Today, a tenth is still covered in ice. Ice sheets can cover very large areas and can be very thick. The world's largest ice sheet covers most of Antarctica and is very slow-moving.

Antarctica covers about 5,400,000 square miles (14,000,000 square km). It is larger in area than either Europe or Australia. However, Antarctica would be the smallest continent if it did not have its ice cap. This icy layer, which averages approximately 7,100 feet (2,200 m) thick, increases Antarctica's surface area and makes Antarctica the highest continent in terms of average elevation.

FACT FILE

Glaciers and ice sheets sometimes give up their secrets centuries later. Thawing ice has revealed the bodies of people who fell into crevasses hundreds of years ago. The ice has preserved their clothes and their internal organs.

WHAT GIVES A RIVER ITS SHAPE?

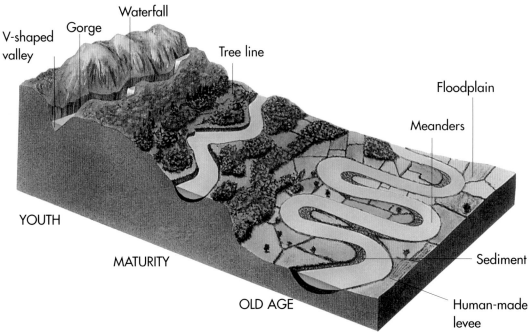

V-shaped valley

Gorge

Waterfall

Tree line

Floodplain

Meanders

YOUTH

MATURITY

OLD AGE

Sediment

Human-made levee

Rivers start on the top of hills as small streams channeling rainfall or as springs releasing ground water. They begin to cut at and change the landscape on the way to the sea. In the highlands, the water can move very quickly and has a lot of power. The river can cut deep gorges and *V*-shaped valleys in softer rocks. In harder rocks, they can form waterfalls. The river moves rocks and pebbles along its bed by bouncing and rolling them. The lighter sediments are carried or dissolved in the water. When the river reaches the more gentle slopes, the river becomes wider and moves slower. Mud and sand is dropped when the river floods and forms ridges along the riverbank. When the river reaches the low plains, it begins to meander.

FACT FILE

The farther a river is from its source on a mountainside, the slower the water travels. This is because the river eventually reaches flatter ground and widens before it reaches the sea.

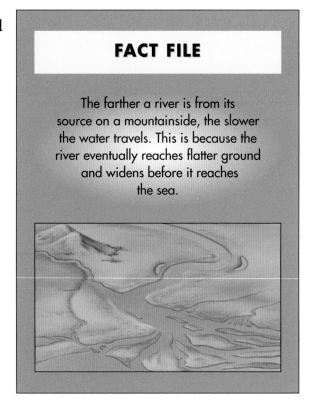

WHAT GIVES A COASTLINE ITS SHAPE?

FACT FILE

Many cliffs on the coast are made up of chalk. Chalk is formed from the skeletons of millions of tiny animals called *foraminifera*. It is a sedimentary rock that formed millions of years ago beneath shallow seas.

Coastlines are constantly changing: they are either being eroded or built up. Waves are very powerful and can remove large amounts of material from a coastline, especially during a storm. The sand and pebbles removed from the coastline are carried by the sea and can be dropped farther along the coast or out to sea.

Many coastal features can be made by the steady erosion of the cliffs and headlands, such as sand dunes, spits, and salt marshes. A beach can make the waves less powerful and reduce the amount of erosion of the coast. Steep cliffs and wave-cut platforms can be formed in areas of hard rock. A bay can be carved out in an area where hard rock has soft rock between it.

SOFT ROCK

Cliff

HARD ROCK

Wave-cut platform

Wave-built terrace

HARD AND SOFT ROCK

Cove

Headland

Arch

Stack

149

WHAT IS CLIMATE?

FACT FILE

Mountains, such as the Rockies in North America, have a typical alpine climate because of their height.

Climatic zones

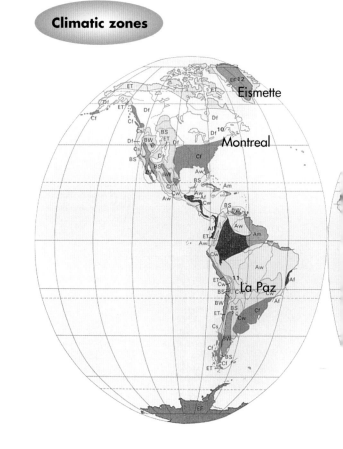

Af	Am	Aw	BS	BW	Cw	Cs
Tropical climates			Dry climates		Warm temperate climates	

Climate is what the weather pattern is like over a long period of time. The seasonal pattern of hot and cold, wet or dry, is averaged over 30 years. The climate is different around the world as the sun does not heat it evenly. The equator gets most of the heat. Winds and ocean currents transport the heat around the earth.

There are four types of climate: tropical, desert (dry), temperate, and polar.

Different areas of the world have different weather patterns. Some areas have a high level of rainfall, while others remain dry. Throughout a year, the weather in a country may change with the seasons.

WHAT IS A SAVANNA?

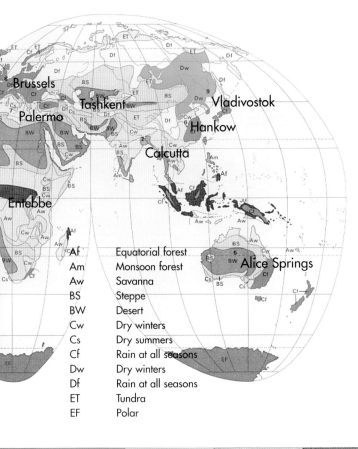

Af	Equatorial forest
Am	Monsoon forest
Aw	Savanna
BS	Steppe
BW	Desert
Cw	Dry winters
Cs	Dry summers
Cf	Rain at all seasons
Dw	Dry winters
Df	Rain at all seasons
ET	Tundra
EF	Polar

Cf	Dw	Df	ET	EF
	Cool temperate climates		Cold climates	

FACT FILE

As well as grazing animals, the African savanna is home to animals that prey on them, such as lions and cheetahs, as well as birds, insects and reptiles.

Savannas are grasslands in areas that have both dry and rainy seasons. These grasslands tend to lie between rain forests and deserts. Most savannas are in the tropics. They cover more than 40 percent of Africa and large areas of India, central South America, and northern Australia. Trees and shrubs are widely scattered on savannas, and their growth is limited by the dry season, during which time no rain may fall for nearly half a year. When the dry season begins, most trees drop their leaves to conserve water and the clumpy grasses die back. Grazing animals, such as zebras and wildebeest, migrate across the savanna to follow the available water.

WHAT IS PRECIPITATION?

Precipitation is simply water falling from clouds and what form it takes depends principally on the air temperature. Rain is precipitation in the form of drops of water. Raindrops form in clouds when microscopic droplets of water condense together. Ice particles of various sizes also form and these may fall as hail, snow, or sleet. In most of Antarctica, it is too cold for anything except snow to fall, whereas in the tropics, almost all precipitation is rain, except in violent storm activity when hail may occur.

Some areas of the world are always too dry and suffer drought, while others get seasonal heavy rains and flooding.

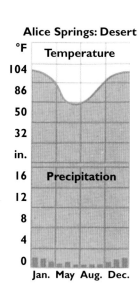

Alice Springs: Desert

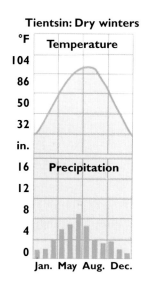

Tientsin: Dry winters

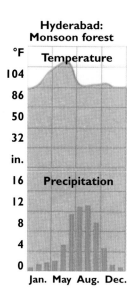

Entebbe: Equatorial forest

Hyderabad: Monsoon forest

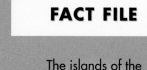

FACT FILE

The islands of the Seychelles are very humid and have high levels of rainfall which feeds the tropical rainforests. The average annual rainfall ranges from 52 inches (132 cm) on some of the coral islands to 92 inches (234 cm) on Mahe.

WHY DOES FLOODING OCCUR?

Flooding occurs when water cannot drain away fast enough in the rivers. In areas of nonporous rocks, water runs off the land very quickly, and streams and rivers soon overflow. Flooding also occurs when winter snows thaw in spring. Huge floods cover parts of Siberia every spring, when snow melts while the rivers are still iced up. Low-lying coastal lands are vulnerable to flooding, especially when gales and high tides cause water to flow inland. Low-lying Bangladesh is particularly susceptible to this kind of flooding. In addition, melting snow in the Himalayan mountains adds a great amount of water to Bangladesh's rivers, increasing the flood risk.

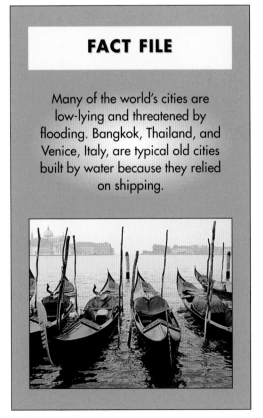

FACT FILE

Many of the world's cities are low-lying and threatened by flooding. Bangkok, Thailand, and Venice, Italy, are typical old cities built by water because they relied on shipping.

WHAT ARE THE MOST EXTREME TEMPERATURES EVER RECORDED?

FACT FILE

One of the animals that has survived Arctic conditions is the polar bear. In very cold climates, animals need excellent insulation to keep their body heat from escaping. This can be in the form of dense hair, fur, or feathers, or by a thick layer of fat or blubber.

Libya and the Antarctic have recorded the most extreme temperatures. The hottest temperature in the shade was in Libya in 1922, when the temperature in the Sahara desert reached 136.4° F (58°C). Temperatures nearly as high as this were recorded in Death Valley in 1913. The coldest temperature ever recorded was in Antarctica in 1983, when Russian scientists measured a low of -128.5° F (–89.2°C). The longest heatwave recorded was in Marble Bar, Australia, when the temperature stayed above 100° F (38°C) for 162 days from October 23, 1923, to April 7, 1924.

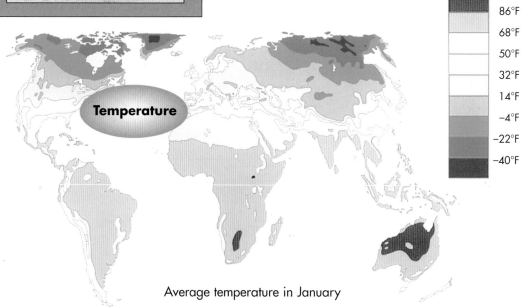

Temperature

86°F
68°F
50°F
32°F
14°F
−4°F
−22°F
−40°F

Average temperature in January

154

WHEN DO DROUGHTS OCCUR?

FACT FILE

An oasis is a fertile area found within a desert. It is a water source in the middle of often vast, dry land.

Drought is a prolonged period–sometimes lasting for years–when less-than-average amounts of rain fall, usually accompanied by higher temperatures than normal. In agricultural areas, the lack of rain and increased heat kill crops. Because the plants are dry, forest and grass fires are more frequent, spread more rapidly, and cover wider areas, sometimes leaving the soil bare and prone to erosion so that even if the rains come again, it is difficult to grow crops. Streams, ponds, and wells often dry up during a drought, and animals may die because of the lack of water. Severe, prolonged droughts, such as those that have occurred in eastern Africa during the past twenty years and more, cause widespread hardship and famine for millions of people.

Rainfall

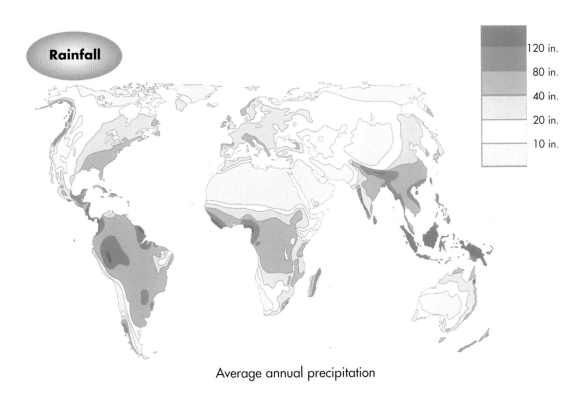

	120 in.
	80 in.
	40 in.
	20 in.
	10 in.

Average annual precipitation

WHAT IS SALINE WATER?

Most of the water on the earth is saline (containing salt) and is found in the oceans. Oceans are a source of food, energy, and minerals. Ships use the oceans to carry cargo between continents. Above all else, the sea helps keep the earth's climate healthy by regulating the air temperature through currents that move hot water from the tropics towards the poles and by supplying the moisture for rainfall. If there were no oceans, life could not exist.

Every natural element can be found in the waters of the oceans. The oceans are especially known for their salt and contain, on average, about 3½ percent salt. Most of this consists of the compound sodium chloride, or ordinary table salt. The levels of salt in the ocean are not uniform: where there is greater evaporation, the water is saltier; while coastal areas near rivers and regions where it rains more are less salty.

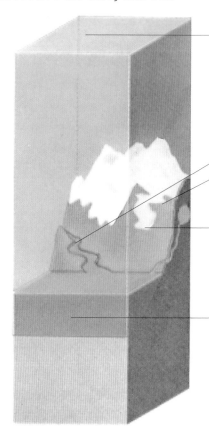

FACT FILE

The salts and other chemicals in the oceans come from a variety of sources. Many originate from rocks dissolved by erosion, while chemicals such as sulphur compounds are also supplied by volcanoes and hydrothermal vents.

WHAT IS IRRIGATION?

Irrigation is the watering of land through artificial methods to lengthen the period when crops can be grown or to extend the area that can be farmed, especially in areas where there is little rainfall for much of the year. The development of civilization in Mesopotamia is thought to have been assisted by their sophisticated irrigation systems that allowed them to achieve better than subsistence-level farming.

In desert regions, such as Egypt and the Arab world, agriculture would not be possible without extensive methods for storing and piping water to where it is needed.

3,120.87 m³

55,275.35 m³

2,073,455.83 m³

7,009,946.75 m³

317,368,137.27 m³

FACT FILE

In the mid-1980s, about 550 million acres (220 million hectares) of land were under irrigation throughout the world. Rice is one of the world's most important food crops. Lowland rice is grown in flat fields that are flooded by irrigation.

WHAT IS THE WATER CYCLE?

In nature, all the world's water circulates from the oceans to the sky, onto the land, and then back to the oceans again in what is called the *water cycle* or *hydrological cycle*. Heat from the sun evaporates water from the oceans, which gradually rises as vapor in the atmosphere. The vaporized water gradually cools and condenses to form clouds, which deposit water back into the oceans or onto the land as rain or snow. The majority falls directly back into the oceans or seas, but some falls on the land and flows back to the seas, completing the cycle, sometimes after periods of thousands of years.

FACT FILE

Fresh water is obtained from two main sources, surface water and ground water. Streams, rivers, and lakes provide surface water, while ground water may be obtained from springs or wells.

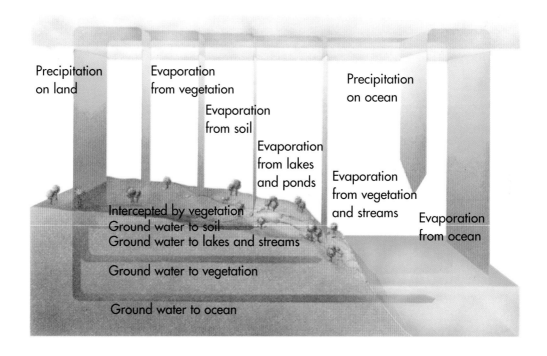

Precipitation on land

Evaporation from vegetation

Evaporation from soil

Precipitation on ocean

Evaporation from lakes and ponds

Evaporation from vegetation and streams

Evaporation from ocean

Intercepted by vegetation
Ground water to soil
Ground water to lakes and streams

Ground water to vegetation

Ground water to ocean

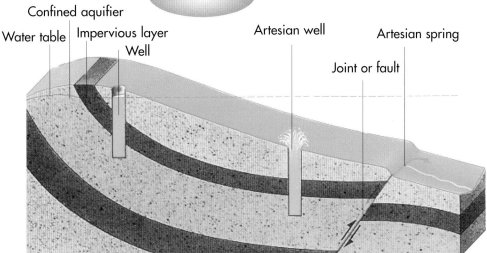

Confined aquifer

Water table

Impervious layer

Well

Artesian well

Artesian spring

Joint or fault

WHAT IS THE WATER TABLE?

The water table is the level of ground water in any one location. It rises slowly after periods of heavy rainfall, although it can take years, for water seeps through soil, cracks in rocks, porous stone, and through beds of sand and gravel. In dry periods, when more water is being used and more is evaporating from vegetation and soil than can be replenished, the water table falls.

An aquifer is a bed of material that holds water, sandwiched between two nonporous layers of rock so that water cannot seep away. Wells are drilled down through the top layer of impervious rock so that the aquifer's ground water can be used. Artesian wells tap into the aquifer in a low part of the bed and use the water's pressure to force itself upwards so there is no need to pump it out of the well.

FACT FILE

Pollution of ground water is a serious problem, especially near cities and industrial sites. Pollutants seep into the ground from contaminated surface water, leaks from sewer pipes and septic tanks, and chemical spills.

WHAT IS A TSUNAMI?

Earthquakes on the ocean floor give a tremendous push to surrounding seawater, creating one or more large, destructive waves called *tsunamis*, or seismic sea waves. Some people call a tsunami a tidal wave, but scientists think the term is misleading because the waves are not caused by the tide.

Tsunamis may reach heights of over 100 ft. (30 m) when they reach shallow water near shore. In the open ocean, tsunamis typically move at speeds of 500 to 600 mph (800 to 970 kmh). They travel great distances while decreasing little in size and can flood coastal areas thousands of miles from their source.

Another form of tsunami is called a *storm surge*. In a storm surge, giant waves are whipped up by the storm. In 1970, a storm surge and cyclone hit Bangladesh, killing 266,000 people. In 1985, another surge killed an additional 10,000 people.

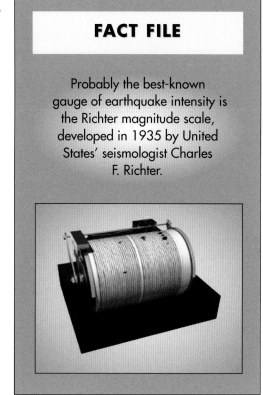

FACT FILE

Probably the best-known gauge of earthquake intensity is the Richter magnitude scale, developed in 1935 by United States' seismologist Charles F. Richter.

WHAT IS AN EYEWALL?

FACT FILE

A hurricane ends quickly if it moves over land. This is because it no longer receives heat energy and moisture from the warm tropical water.

A tropical storm achieves hurricane status when its winds exceed 74 mph (119 kph). By the time a storm reaches hurricane intensity, it usually has a well-developed center, or eye, at its middle. Surface pressure drops to its lowest point in this eye. In the eyewall, or eye, of the storm, warm air spirals upward, creating the hurricane's strongest winds. The speed is related to the diameter of the eye. Just as ice skaters spin faster when they pull their arms into their bodies so a hurricane's winds blow faster if its eye is small and compact. If the eye begins to widen, the wind decreases.

Heavy rains fall from the eyewall and from bands of dense clouds that swirl around it. These bands, called *rainbands*, can produce more than two inches (5 cm) of rain per hour. Tornados are violently rotating columns of air that travel over land, instead of water. Tornados descend from the base of thunderclouds to the ground. The windspeeds can reach 250 mph (400 kph), and the path of damage caused by a tornado can be as much as 1 mile (2 km) wide.

WHAT IS ACID RAIN?

FACT FILE

Adding lime to lakes and rivers temporarily neutralizes their acidity caused by acid rain. It is not known whether this may have harmful side effects.

Acid rain is rain, snow, or sleet that has been polluted by acids. Increased acidity upsets the delicate pH balance of fresh water, and kills insects, fish, and other wildlife that depend on lakes, rivers, and streams. High concentrations of acid rain can harm forests, burning the trees' leaves and changing the acidity of soil, which makes it difficult for plants to thrive. The plants become less resistant to disease and many die.

Acid rain is a problem of the Industrial Age, resulting mainly from the burning of fossil fuels in power stations and factories, as well as cars and other vehicles. The resulting compounds, for example sulphur dioxide and nitrogen oxides, react with vapor in the atmosphere to create such compounds as sulphuric and nitric acid.

Large parts of eastern North America, central Europe, Scandinavia, and parts of Asia have been badly affected by acid rain. Acts forcing companies to reduce their emissions of such compounds have been enforced in many western countries for some years now. The levels of acidity are beginning to drop, but this has not yet happened worldwide.

WHY DOES DEFORESTATION OCCUR?

The world's rain forests are rapidly disappearing. More than half of this area has been irretrievably destroyed by humans. The primary causes are land clearance for agriculture, commercial logging of tropical hardwoods, and destructive open-cast mining for chemicals. Large areas have also been lost to hydroelectric projects.

FACT FILE

Rain forests benefit people in four major ways. They provide economic, scientific, environmental, and recreational value.

In the last few years of the twentieth century, forest clearance in Indonesia caused extensive forest fires. Smoke blanketed much of southeast Asia for months.

Unfortunately, rain forest species such as the orangutan are in danger of becoming extinct because their habitat is being destroyed. When large areas of forest are cleared and only isolated patches are left, there are not large enough areas for them to live in. Scientists estimate that more than 7,000 species, including insects, reptiles, and mammals, become extinct each year due to tropical deforestation.

HOW BIG ARE ASTEROIDS?

Asteroids are small rocky or icy bodies that orbit the sun. There are more than 100,000 asteroids in orbit. Some measure less than half a mile (1km) across, while the largest known is 630 miles (1,000 km). Only a few of them have a diameter greater than 19 miles (30 km). They are sometimes called minor planets. Most asteroids are found in an orbit between Mars and Jupiter, called the *asteroid belt*. More than 7,000 of these have been identified. The asteroid belt may be the shattered remains of a planet destroyed by Jupiter's enormous gravity or perhaps one that was prevented from forming. There are also asteroids in orbits near the earth as well as Jupiter.

One asteroid, called Ida, has a tiny moon of its own, Dactyl. This is the smallest known body in the solar system to have a satellite. Astronomers believe that the asteroids were probably formed at the same time as the planets from the dust cloud that surrounded the sun when it was young.

The Asteroid Belt

FACT FILE

Many asteroids have already struck the earth and the resulting craters have been studied extensively by geologists. Some scientists believe that such an impact near Mexico 65 million years ago caused the extinction of the dinosaurs.

HOW ARE METEORITES FORMED?

Meteorites are made of rock or metal and may have been formed at the same time as the solar system. Meteorites may be debris from impacts between other small bodies and planets such as Mars. They enter the earth's atmosphere at speeds of 6.9 mps (11 kms), which makes them glow as they vaporize. Several thousand meteoroids enter the earth's atmosphere every year, but few reach the ground. Technically, meteoroids are called *meteorites* only if they actually hit the earth.

The largest known meteorite is made of iron and weighs 65 tons (66 tonnes). It probably fell to the earth during prehistoric times in the area now known as Namibia, in southwest Africa.

It is very hard to find meteorites. Recently, researchers have found them on the ice sheets in the Arctic and the Antarctic, where they are easier to locate.

On planets and moons that have no atmosphere, large numbers of meteorites strike with enormous power. Our own moon is estimated to have 3,000,000 meteorite craters measuring 1 mile (2 km) or more in diameter. Meteorite craters are rare on the earth because our atmosphere slows the meteoroid and usually burns it up before it hits the ground.

FACT FILE

An enormous meteorite caused a huge impact crater at Wolf Creek in Australia. The amount of energy the impact released would have been equivalent to hundreds of nuclear weapons.

WHAT IS A FALLING STAR?

"Falling stars" appear as faint streaks of light in the night sky. Today, we know that they are not stars but meteors. Meteors are small, solid bodies, some only the size of dust particles, that travel through space and may hit the earth's atmosphere.

Hundreds of thousands meteors collide with the earth's atmosphere daily but we see most of them only when they leave fiery trails of light. If the meteors measure more than ¼ inch (8 mm) across, they vaporize because of frictional heating and cause ionized trails in the upper atmosphere. Larger bodies may penetrate deeper and then blow up as a fireball.

Meteor showers occur when the earth is at specific places in its orbit, and are believed to be caused by material from the tails of comets.

The Milky Way

FACT FILE

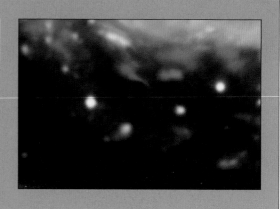

Sometimes it is difficult to see the stars. The stars are still there, but there may be clouds covering the night sky. Artificial lights from our homes and street lighting, referred to as *ground clutter*, make it too light to see the stars.

HOW DO STARS MAKE PICTURES?

For many thousands of years people all over the world have noticed patterns in the stars and have given them names. These groups are called *constellations* which comes from the Latin word for "star," *stella*.

Many of the constellations we know today are derived from the ancient Babylonians, who named some of their star pictures after animals and royal and mythological figures. Their knowledge was handed down to the Greeks and from them passed to the Romans, who both attached their own heroes and gods to the star patterns. We still use their names for many of the constellations we see today. For example, Ursa Major is the great bear, Ursa Minor is the little bear, Cancer is the crab, and Aries is the ram. Later, astronomers added more constellations, mainly in the southern part of the sky, including Microscopium, the microscope, and Carina, the keel. Today astronomers recognize 88 constellations.

FACT FILE

Halley's Comet returns to the inner solar system every 76 years after it traveles out close to the orbit of Pluto. Its last encounter with earth was in 1986.

HOW MUCH DOES THE ATMOSPHERE WEIGH?

The earth is surrounded by a thick blanket of about 20 gases, composed mainly of nitrogen and oxygen, called the *atmosphere*. It also contains water vapor and dust particles. It is densest closest to the ground and thins progressively as it is higher.

Air, like all matter, has weight. Scientists have calculated that our atmosphere weighs 5,100,000,000,000,000 tons (5,170,000,000,000,000 tonnes)!

So why don't we feel the weight of all this air pressing down on us and against us? We are not aware of this pressure because our bodies are designed to live with this pressure. Higher up in the atmosphere, pressure is less, which is why aircraft cabins have to be pressurized. Similarly, pressure increases rapidly with depth in the oceans, so divers can reach only the very top levels of the water without the protection of submarines.

The earth's atmosphere enables it to support life. Chemicals in it protect us from the sun's rays and it prevents all but the biggest meteorites hitting the surface. Without atmosphere, the oceans would evaporate and sea life would die.

FACT FILE

Beneath the land and water that cover the earth's surface lie layers of rock and metal that carry very high temperatures. The deepest mines ever dug have not reached the bottom of the outer layer, called the *crust*. Under the crust is a layer of partly solid and partly molten rock.

HOW OLD IS THE EARTH?

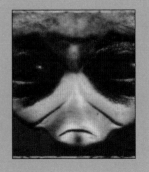

The earth began to form over 4.5 billion years ago, but for millions of years it was too hot to support life. About 3.6 billion years ago, scientists think that a body the size of Mars crashed into the young earth, causing the formation of the moon. Gradually, the earth's crust cooled and the oceans and atmosphere formed. But how do we know this? The earth's geological record does not go back that far, so the answer is based on theory.

To find the age of the earth it was necessary to find out how the sun and all the planets came into being. There are several different theories to explain this.

One theory is called *nebular hypothesis*, which dates to the eighteenth century. This theory holds that a mass of white-hot gas whirled about in space getting smaller and hotter all the time, throwing off rings of gas which condensed to form a planet. Another theory, the *planetismal hypothesis* dates to the 1920s. The theory is that the gravitation of a large star pulled on the sun and caused it to eject filaments of plasma that condensed into tiny bodies, which eventually grew into planets. The current theory is that as the sun formed, a broad disk of dust and gas condensed around it. Material within this disk began to clump together and eventually accreted into the nine planets.

FACT FILE

No one has ever proved that life exists on other planets. However, as there are billions of stars, some with planets, it seems unlikely that the earth is the only place with the right conditions for life. Astronomers use radio telescopes to search for messages from other civilizations.

WHY DON'T PLANETS COLLIDE?

Sometimes, the planets look very close together in the sky, and you might wonder if they are ever going to collide.

Within the solar system, astronomers use a system of measurements they call *astronomical units* to measure space. It's a useful way to explore the relative distances of the planets from the sun. An astronomical unit (AU) is the mean distance of the earth from the eun. Of the inner planets, Mercury's mean distance from the sun is 0.387 AU, a little over a third of the way between the sun and earth. Venus is 0.723 AU, almost three-quarters of the way to the earth.

Mars orbits at 1.524 AU, Jupiter at 5.203 AU, Saturn at 9.539 AU, Uranus at 19.182 AU, Neptune at 30.958 AU, and Pluto at 39.44 AU. These are mean distances because none of the planets have a circular orbit. So, sometimes, a planet is closer to or farther out from the sun than these figures suggest. In fact, Pluto's orbit is far from circular. It can come as close as 29.66 AU or as far as 49.54 AU. Although Pluto is sometimes closer to the sun than Neptune, their orbits never meet. So there is no danger of them, or any other of the planets, colliding.

FACT FILE

Mars is known as the "Red Planet" because it is covered by a stony desert that contains iron oxide, making it appear a rusty-red color. At one time, Mars had an atmosphere containing oxygen and valleys through which water may have flowed.

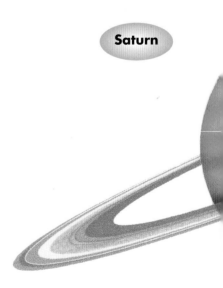

Saturn

How was the light-year discovered?

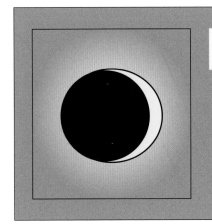

FACT FILE

In a lunar eclipse, the earth lies directly between the sun and moon, blocking off direct light to the moon, so that the latter seems to vanish. Some light reaches the moon through the earth's atmosphere, so the eclipsed moon sometimes appears dark red.

Neptune

Although we cannot fully explain light, we can measure it quite accurately, and we have a fairly good idea how fast it travels. This was done by a Danish astronomer named Olaus Römer in 1676. In the early twentieth century, Professor Albert Michelson spent years trying to determine the exact speed of light. He arrived at a speed of 186,284 miles (299,796 km) per second in the atmosphere. This was astonishingly accurate. The currently accepted figure is 186,281.79 miles (299,792.5 km) per second through a vacuum, where light travels faster.

If we multiply this speed by the number of seconds in a year, we would find that light travels 5,880,000,000,000 miles (9,460,700,000,000 km) in a year. This distance is called a *light-year*.

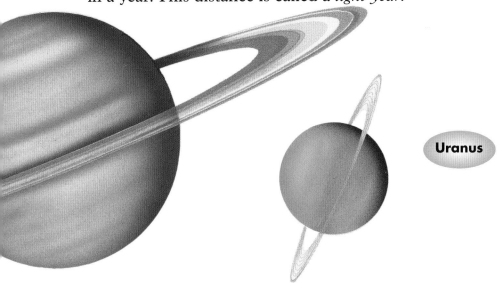

Uranus

HOW FAR DOES OUTER SPACE GO?

The simple answer to this question is that nobody knows. We don't have strong enough telescopes to see all of the way to the edge of space. Astronomers picture the whole universe as extending much farther in all directions. But how far? Is there an edge or not?

Astronomers think that the shape of space may provide the answer. Some have calculated what radiation left over from the early universe should appear like in instruments if space curves round on itself. This appears to be the case. This complicated curvature implies that it is impossible to travel beyond space. However, not all astronomers agree with the results of these calculations. Some think that the universe may be infinite.

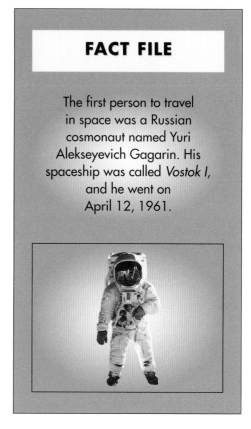

FACT FILE

The first person to travel in space was a Russian cosmonaut named Yuri Alekseyevich Gagarin. His spaceship was called *Vostok I*, and he went on April 12, 1961.

A black hole

HOW FAST DOES THE EARTH MOVE?

The earth has two main motions. It spins on its axis once every 23 hours, 56 minutes, and 4.091 seconds. It also moves in an orbit around the sun once every 365¼ days.

It was believed that the speed of the rotation never changed, but there are tiny variations. Our day is getting longer by about one-thousandth of a second per century.

Like all of the planets, the earth moves faster when it is closer to the sun (perihelion) than it does when farther out (aphelion). At aphelion, the earth orbits the sun at 18.2 (29.12 kms) and at perihelion it is travelling at at speed of 18.8 mps (30.8 kms)

FACT FILE

Human beings have a built-in body clock and normally have a good idea of the time even without the use of clocks. Our body is aware of the amount of time that has passed since daybreak.

HOW BIG IS THE UNIVERSE?

Astronomers think that the universe formed about 13 billion years ago, but calculations of its size are too mind-numbing for most of us.

The earth is only a tiny member in our solar system. The light from the brightest star in the sky, Sirius, takes over 8½ years to get here. The solar system lies in a quiet backwater of an average galaxy that contains perhaps 100,000,000 stars. It is part of a local group of 40-odd galaxies, some members of which are almost 2,500,000 light-years away. Beyond vast empty tracts of space, larger clusters of galaxies can be detected. The Virgo supercluster contains more than 3,000 galaxies.

FACT FILE

More than two-thirds of the earth's surface is covered by seas and oceans. This means that about 72 percent of the earth's surface is water. This water is either in the oceans, locked away as ice at the poles or held as water vapor in the atmosphere. All of the earth's water is known as the hydrosphere.

WHAT IS THE EARTH MADE OF ?

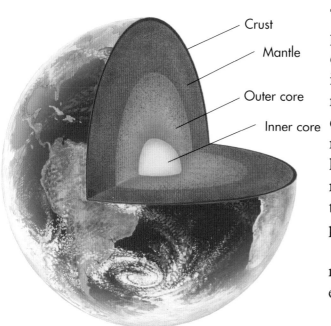

Crust

Mantle

Outer core

Inner core

The earth is an almost spherical planet and is made up of several distinct layers. The solid inner core is thought to consist mainly of nickel and iron. The liquid outer core has a similar composition. The relative motions of the solid and liquid parts of the core and movements within them are thought to produce the earth's protective magnetic field.

Above the outer core is the mantle, which is slowly moving, even though it is solid rock.

Above the mantle lies the lithosphere. The outer layer of the lithosphere is the crust. The high parts of this crust are the continents, and the low parts of it hold the waters of the oceans, seas, and lakes.

The heat radiating out from the center of the planet and the currents in the mantle drive the forces that give us volcanoes and replenish the gases in the atmosphere. Without them, there would be no atmosphere, no oceans, and no life on our planet.

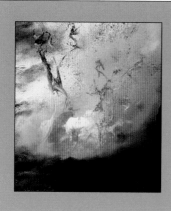

FACT FILE

Volcanoes are openings in the earth's crust through which molten lava, red-hot rocks, steam, and fumes pour out. Most volcanoes have a single central pipe through which lava reaches the surface, building up into a cone as it cools. This consists of layers of lava and volcanic ash with a crater at the center. Active volcanoes smoke and spit out lava.

HOW ARE STARS FORMED?

A star is a huge ball of bright, hot ionized gas called *plasma*. The main source of fuel for most of a star's life is hydrogen, which it converts into helium. They also contain other chemical elements, such as nitrogen, oxygen, iron, nickel, and zinc.

Stars come into existence in the vast, cold clouds of dust and gas that astronomers refer to as stellar nurseries. They are not particularly dense but are a lot denser than the vacuum of space. If there is a disturbance in a bit of the cloud, perhaps as the result of a nearby star exploding, some of the particles might clump together. As they do, they will spin together and slowly attract more particles. As the group gradually gets larger and larger, its spins faster, and its gravitational attraction becomes greater.

Pressure also builds up within the ball, which increases its heat. Eventually, when the pressure and temperature inside the ball become very high, about 15 million °C, nuclear reactions take place in the core, and the gas ball becomes a star. The larger a star, the faster it will use up its hydrogen. Some massive stars last only tens of thousands of years before exploding, while small stars like our sun last for tens of millions of years.

FACT FILE

A nebula is an enormous mass of gas and solid material that appears to be solid. However, it is mostly composed of dust and gas, which slowly condenses into stars.

How Far Away Are the Stars?

The sun is about 93,000,000 miles from the earth. As light travels at the rate of 186,000 mps (299,792,458 kps), it takes eight minutes for the light to reach us. The next closest stars to earth are Proxima Centauri and Alpha Centauri. They are 270,000 times farther away from the earth than the sun. This means that it would take their light 4½ years to reach the earth. Other stars are unimaginably far away. Betelgeuse, the red star in Orion's shoulder, is approximately 427 light-years away.

To measure the distance of very nearby stars, astronomers use a form of geometry. Close stars appear to move very slightly against the background stars over the earth's annual orbit. If measurements are taken at each extreme, perhaps in December and June, the angle between the two points can be used to calculate its distance.

Other techniques are used for measuring the distances to more remote stars and galaxies, involving the use of spectroscopy–the analysis of the chemistry of stars through their light.

FACT FILE

The Milky Way is a huge mass of gas and stars that can be clearly seen as a band of light across the night sky. The earth, and everything else in the solar system is part of the Milky Way.

OTHER

FACTS

CONTENTS

HOW DO PLANTS SURVIVE IN THE DESERT? 180
HOW LONG CAN A CAMEL GO WITHOUT WATER? 181

HOW DO FERNS REPRODUCE? 182
HOW DO MUSHROOMS GROW? 183

HOW DO MAMMALS DIFFER FROM OTHER ANIMALS? 184
HOW ENDANGERED ARE PANDAS? 185

WHEN DO PONDS AND LAKES BECOME POLLUTED? 186
WHEN DOES PHOTOSYNTHESIS OCCUR? 187

WHAT ARE PRIMATES? 188
WHAT IS THE ADVANTAGE OF BEING WARM-BLOODED? 189

WHAT DO BIRDS EAT? 190
WHAT ARE FEATHERS MADE OF? 191

WHAT ARE MOLLUSKS? 192
WHAT ARE ARTHROPODS? 193

HOW ARE MOUNTAINS FORMED? 194
HOW DOES RAIN CAUSE ROCKSLIDES? 195

HOW ARE VOLCANOES FORMED? 196
HOW DO VOLCANOES ERUPT? 197

HOW DOES RAIN FALL? 198
HOW DOES PRESSURE AFFECT OUR WEATHER? 199

HOW DOES AIR BECOME POLLUTED? 200
HOW CAN AEROSOLS DAMAGE THE EARTH? 201

WHEN ARE FUNGI EDIBLE? 202
WHEN DO WE SEE FAIRY RINGS? 203

HOW WAS PENICILLIN DISCOVERED? 204
HOW DO BACTERIA AND VIRUSES DIFFER? 205

HOW DO PARASITES LIVE? 206
HOW ARE SWARMS OF LOCUST FORMED? 207

WHAT IS POLLEN? 208
WHAT ARE LICHENS? 209

WHAT IS AN INVERTEBRATE? 210
WHAT ARE ALGAE? 211

WHAT ARE PLANTS USED FOR? 212
WHAT ARE UMBELS? 213

WHAT IS CONSERVATION? 214
WHAT IS A CRUSTACEAN? 215

WHAT IS A MARSUPIAL? 216
WHAT IS A REPTILE? 217

WHAT IS A PECKING ORDER? 218
WHAT IS THE FOOD CHAIN? 219

WHAT ARE NETTLES? 220
WHAT IS A WEED? 221

WHAT IS THE TALLEST TREE IN THE WORLD? 222
WHAT ARE MUSSELS? 223

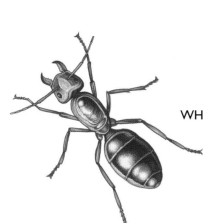

HOW DO PLANTS SURVIVE IN THE DESERT?

There are many kinds of deserts. Some deserts are familiar, with bare rock, shifting sand, and the hot sun beating down. Others, such as the Gobi, have bitterly cold winters. So, a desert is a region where only special forms of life can exist, and they have adapted themselves accordingly.

A good example of a desert life form is the cactus. The cactus has adapted extremely well to hot, arid conditions. Cactuses have thick, fleshy stems, which store water. Little or no leaf surface prevents too much evaporation of water from the plant's surface. Many desert plants have thorns, spines, or a horrible taste and smell which discourages animals from eating them.

Desert plants usually lie dormant during the dry or cool season or drop seeds that can survive such a period.

FACT FILE

When a rock is exposed to the action of wind, rain, and frost, it breaks up into smaller particles. If the particles are small enough, these particles are then called *sand*.

A desert cactus

180

HOW LONG CAN A CAMEL GO WITHOUT WATER?

The most important part of the camel is its hump. This is where a camel stores food. When the hump is empty, it loses its firm shape and flops to one side.

The camel can also carry its own water supply. The camel has three stomachs. Contrary to popular belief, the camel does not store water in its hump but in muscular pockets in the walls of the first two stomachs. When the camel wants water, the muscles relax to release as much as is needed.

It is perhaps surprising to learn that camels can only last for a maximum of ten days without water. This is why oases hidden in the deserts of north Africa and Arabia have always been very important to traders and nomads. They can allow their animals to stock up on more water regularly there.

FACT FILE

Plants can also store food and water during the winter or in very dry conditions. Underground storage organs develop from roots, stem, or leaf bases. The Venus flytrap has a trap, which looks and smells like a flower to insects. When insects land on it, they touch a trigger hair, which slams the trap shut. They are then digested by the plant.

HOW DO FERNS REPRODUCE?

Ferns do not reproduce in the same way as other plants. They have fronds instead of true leaves. Some ferns grow into a tree-like form that can be 80 ft. (24 m) tall.

Microscopic spores are produced on the underside of the ferns' fronds. These spores are scattered by the wind. When these spores land in a suitably damp place, they will sprout and grow into a tiny flat plant that develops small reproductive structures.

Sperm fertilizes the egg cell, which then begins to grow as the tiny plant shrivels up and dies. This is when the complete fern begins to develop.

The fern's reproductive parts are very delicate and can only survive in a moist atmosphere. So, these plants will only grow in damp places.

FACT FILE

Algae are the most primitive form of plant life. Most algae are aquatic and range in size from microscopic single-celled organisms to seaweed that is several yards long. Algae do not have roots but cling on to structures with an organ called a *hold-fast*.

HOW DO MUSHROOMS GROW?

Mushrooms are part of the fungus family, along with toadstools.
The part of the mushroom that you see above the ground is the fruiting body. Most of these only appear during autumn. The main part of the plant consists of a dense mat of tangled white threads. These threads are known as mycelium or spawn.

If allowed to mature, mushrooms will develop tiny spores on the gills underneath the cap. When ripe, they come loose and blow away in the wind. Mushroom spores are tiny and can travel great distances. When a spore lands in suitable ground, it will eventually develop into a new mycelium thread. The fruiting bodies are produced from buds of tissue that push up through the soil to form the next generation of fruiting bodies. Some mushrooms grow in clumps, while others, such as puffballs, grow in circles commonly known as fairy rings.

FACT FILE

Lichens are peculiar organisms in which algae and fungi both live together. Many grow like a mat, while others look like a small branched plant. They often grow on roofs, rocks, or tree branches and are frequently brightly colored.

A Siberian tiger

HOW DO MAMMALS DIFFER FROM OTHER ANIMALS?

Mammals are vertebrate animals that nourish their young with milk. All mammals are warm-blooded. At some stage in their development, mammals will grow hair, although sometimes they are born without any at all.

Mammals all give birth to live young, which are smaller versions of the adult animal.

There is an unusual group of Australian mammals, called *monotremes*, that actually lay eggs. The echidnas, or spiny anteaters, are monotremes. So are the duck-billed platypuses. Shrews are the smallest kind of mammal. The largest living land mammal is the African elephant.

FACT FILE

The duck-billed platypus has a leathery bill shaped like a duck's beak, a body similar to an otter, and a tail very much like a beaver's. To make things even stranger, it has poisonous spurs on its legs, too!

How endangered are pandas?

FACT FILE

Millions of African elephants have been hunted down and killed by poachers for their ivory tusks. These elephants are becoming an endangered species.

Although pandas have never existed in great numbers, farming has now destroyed much of their natural habitat in China. Due to shortage of food, there are now fewer than 1,000 giant pandas remaining.

Human beings have accelerated the extinction of many more animals by changing the animal's environments so rapidly that the animals do not have time to adapt. One example of this is the destruction of the Indonesian rainforest, which has left nowhere for the orangutan to live. Hunting is another reason for the reduced number of animals, such as tigers, and the probable extinction of others.

WHEN DO PONDS AND LAKES BECOME POLLUTED?

Many years ago, the greatest threat to areas of standing water, such as ponds and lakes, was neglect. They gradually filled in and were occupied by shrubs and trees. Today, however, pollution from the modern world is the most serious threat to all water life. Some farming practices pollute the water with fertilizers and pesticides. Sometimes, sewage and waste from industry is also discharged into the rivers. On top of this, rivers and canals are often used as unofficial dumping sites for household waste. Tough laws may make pollution a thing of the past.

FACT FILE

Frogs produce large quantities of spawn in the spring. Keep a small amount in a jar with pond weeds and watch it grow into tadpoles.

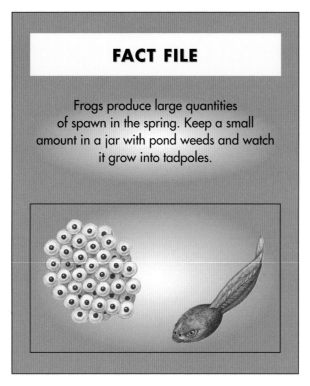

WHEN DOES PHOTOSYNTHESIS OCCUR?

Photosynthesis is the process by which green plants and other certain organisms transform light energy into chemical energy. During photosynthesis, light energy is captured and used to convert water, carbon dioxide, and minerals into oxygen and energy-rich organic compounds.

The plant contains packets of a green pigment called *chlorophyll* that carries out this process. During photosynthesis, water and carbon dioxide from the air are converted into sugars that nourish the plant. At the same time, the plant releases oxygen into the air.

FACT FILE

The process of photosynthesis takes place mostly in the leaves of a plant. Leaves are large and flat so that a large area is exposed to sunlight.

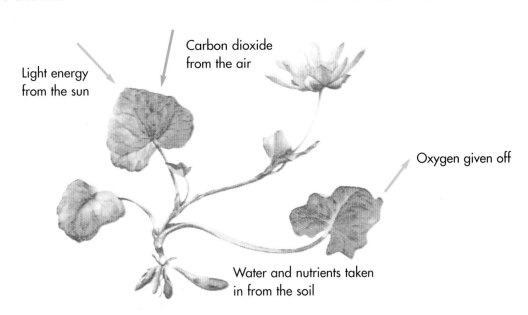

Light energy from the sun

Carbon dioxide from the air

Oxygen given off

Water and nutrients taken in from the soil

WHAT ARE PRIMATES?

There are about 180 different species of primate. Most primates live in the tropical regions of the world. The most numerous primate is the Homo sapiens, or human beings. All primates have fairly large brains and forward-facing eyes that enable them to judge distances accurately. Instead of claws or hoofs, like other mammals, primates have fingers and toes with soft, sensitive tips. They also have the ability to grasp with their fingers, thumbs, and toes.

The largest primate is the gorilla. A male gorilla can weigh up to 605 lb. (275 kg). The smallest is the mouse lemur, which has a total body length of only 6 inches (15 cm).

Baby orangutan

FACT FILE

The gibbon is a small ape found in Indo-Malayan forests. Gibbons, unlike the great apes, have elongated arms and hard, calloused skin on their buttocks. They have canine teeth and live in trees.

WHAT IS THE ADVANTAGE OF BEING WARM-BLOODED?

Warm-blooded animals are able to maintain their own body temperatures regardless of the temperatures around them. The animals with warm blood are birds and mammals. Almost all other animals are cold-blooded, which means that they rely on their surroundings for warmth. Being warm-blooded means that an animal produces heat from food and from physical activity. Some young warm-blooded animals, such as human children and chicks, do not develop this mechanism straight away, which is why most birds brood their young. One of the primary advantages of being warm-blooded is that an animal can start looking for food as soon as it is light, rather than having to wait for the sun to warm its body.

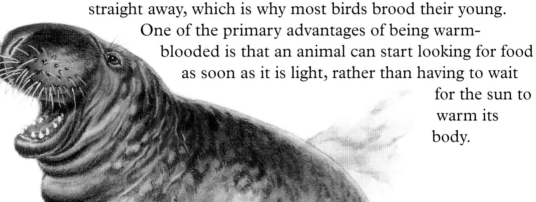

FACT FILE

Some warm-blooded animals must hibernate during cold seasons to reduce their need for food and to protect themselves from the cold. These include mammals such as bats, chipmunks, hamsters, squirrels, hedgehogs, lemurs, and marmots.

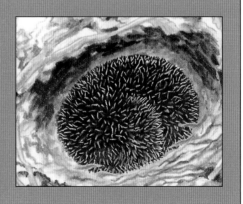

WHAT DO BIRDS EAT?

Different species of birds have different diets, just as mammals do. Some birds are vegetarians, eating fruits and seeds. Others feed on insects and other invertebrates, such as worms. Birds' beaks are adapted to the kind of food they eat. The beaks of meat-eaters are often hooked and sharp, ideal for tearing flesh from carcasses. Birds that search for food along the seashore or on mud banks often have long pointed beaks for burrowing into soft ground. It is fascinating to watch sea birds dive into the water. Gannets, for example, plunge in head-first with folded wings in a lower slanting dive. They disappear deep underwater, often with a splash of spray.

Another bird with an interesting feeding pattern is the swift or martin. They are insect-eaters and feed on the wing. They can be seen circling above water to catch their prey.

FACT FILE

Bald eagles pluck fish out of the water with their talons, and sometimes, they follow seabirds as a means of locating fish. Besides live fish, bald eagles prey on other birds, small mammals, snakes, turtles, and crabs.

Goldcrest

Falcon

WHAT ARE FEATHERS MADE OF?

Feathers consist of beta keratin, which is a form of protein. They are considered to have evolved from reptilian scales. Beta keratin can also be found in hair, hoofs, and fingernails. Feathers are periodically molted, or shed, and other keratinized structures, such as bills and claws, may be molted as well. Specialized nerve endings are present throughout the skin. A preen gland is located on the back just in front of the tail and secretes oil for grooming the feathers. This gland is most pronounced in aquatic birds to ensure that their feathers are waterproof. The many different types of feathers are designed for insulation, flight, formation of body contours, display, and sensory reception. Unlike the hair of most mammals, feathers do not cover the entire skin surface of birds but are arranged in symmetrical tracts with areas of bare skin.

FACT FILE

Penguins have feathers, but they cannot fly. They can swim at great speed using their wings as flippers to power them in the water.

WHAT ARE MOLLUSKS?

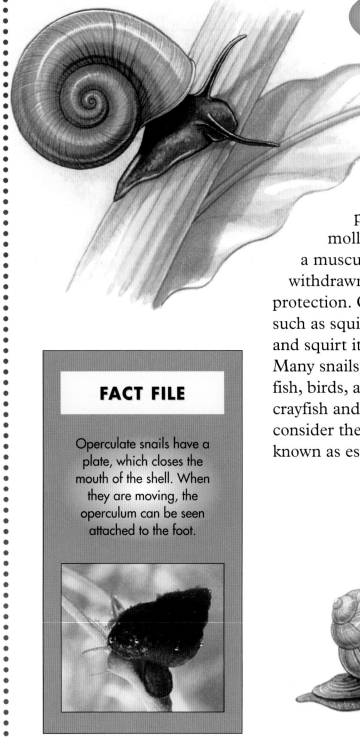

Great ramshorn snail

After insects, mollusks form the largest group of animals. Mollusks have soft, muscular bodies, often covered by a protective shell. Some mollusks, such as snails, move on a muscular foot, which can be withdrawn into the shell for protection. Other sea-dwelling mollusks, such as squid and scallops, take in water and squirt it out to jet-propel themselves. Many snails are an important food for fish, birds, and crustaceans, such as crayfish and lobsters. Many people consider the Helix garden snail, which is known as escargot, a great delicacy.

FACT FILE

Operculate snails have a plate, which closes the mouth of the shell. When they are moving, the operculum can be seen attached to the foot.

Freshwater winkle

WHAT ARE ARTHROPODS?

Arthropods are animals with a hard external skeleton like a suit of armor. The skeleton is jointed to allow movement. Arthropods have evolved differently than vertebrates. Even their blood is chemically different, and so, it is not red. They do not have a brain and spinal cord like vertebrates.

Instead, they have a nerve cord running along the underside of their body and small thickenings of this nerve cord instead of a brain. Arthropods have efficient eyes, but these work in a different way from those of vertebrates. Arthropods, such as spiders, may have many eyes.

Ant

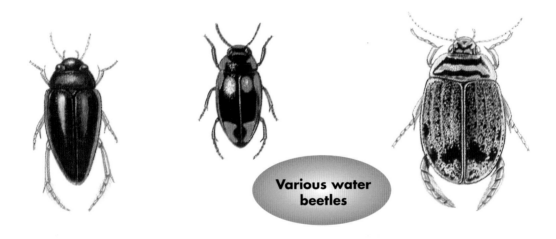

Various water beetles

FACT FILE

The most important groups of arthropods are the following: (1) insects; (2) crustaceans (including this red-banded sea shrimp); (3) arachnids; (4) chilopods or centipedes; and (5) diplopods or millipedes.

HOW ARE MOUNTAINS FORMED?

Most mountains are formed on the earth as a result of plate tectonics. It is a ongoing process. For example, the Himalayan mountains are still being lifted as India moves north.

There are a variety of types of mountains. Folded mountains are made of rock layers that have been crumpled by great pressure into large folds. There are various types of folded mountains defined by the rock types, the shape of the folds, and whether the rocks have subsequently fractured.

Volcanoes can occur where the earth's crustal plates are sliding against each other, causing great frictional heat. Volcanoes also occur over hotspots in thin oceanic plates. The Hawaiian islands are examples of the latter. Dome mountains are caused by pressure from surrounding regions or from molten lava underneath.

Block mountains occur when faults repeatedly rupture catastrophically. Huge parts of the surface, including entire blocks of rocks are raised above their surroundings.

FACT FILE

Glaciers are large masses of ice that form on land and move slowly under their own weight. Glaciers have shaped most of the world's highest mountains, carving out huge valleys.

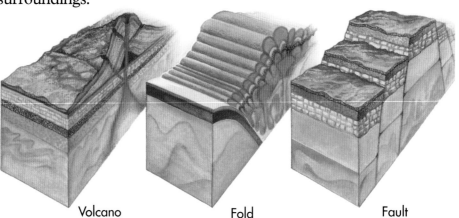

Volcano   Fold   Fault

HOW DOES RAIN CAUSE ROCKSLIDES?

Often times, there are rockslides after heavy rain. This is because the rainwater enters cracks in the rock. When it freezes, the water expands and opens the crack wider. As the thaw starts, the pieces of rock splinter and separate from the main rock. Loose rock is continuously building up on a mountainside, but it is normally only the small pieces that slide down. This loose, broken rock is called *scree*. A rockslide will take place when a mass of this broken rock slides down the side of a mountain, mixed with a torrent of mud.

FACT FILE

As water vapor builds up in the winds blown towards mountains, it is forced to rise, and the temperature drops. The water condenses into clouds at these higher altitudes. This is why mountain peaks are often surrounded by layers of cloud.

HOW ARE VOLCANOES FORMED?

FACT FILE

Boiling water is blasted out of the ground by a geyser. When the hot water emerges, it forms a hot spring. In some countries, they use these springs for heating purposes.

Secondary vent

Layers of ash and lava

Volcanoes are formed because the temperature under the surface of the earth becomes hotter and hotter the deeper you go down. At a depth of about twenty miles, it is hot enough to melt most rocks.

When rock melts, it expands and needs more space. In some areas of the world, mountains are being uplifted. The pressure is not very strong under these rising mountain ranges, and so a reservoir of melted rock known as "magma" may form underneath them.

This molten rock rises in the cracks formed by the uplift. When the pressure in the reservoir becomes greater than the roof of rock over it, it bursts out as a volcano. During the eruption, hot gaseous liquid, or solid material, is blown out. The material piles up around the opening, and a cone-shaped mound is formed. This is the result of a volcano.

In February, 1943, in the middle of a cornfield in Mexico, people saw a rare and amazing event occur. A volcano was being born! In three months, it had formed a cone about 1,000 ft. (300 m) high.

HOW DO VOLCANOES ERUPT?

Gas and ashes

Main vent

Lava

FACT FILE

The edges of the Pacific plate are surrounded by volcanic activity. Earthquakes and hot springs are caused by the shifting of the crust and hot lava rising near the surface. There is even a volcano in the cold waters of the Antarctic.

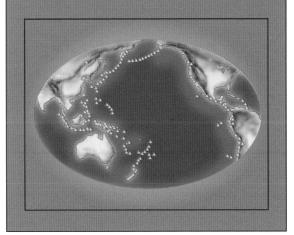

In the center of a volcano is a mass of molten rock. When it reaches the surface, it is known as lava. Its temperature can be as high as 2200° F (1,200°C). Lava can be as runny as water or so thick that it scarcely moves at all. When the pressure in the center of the volcano becomes too great, it simply erupts. It hurls out masses of dust, rocks, ash, steam, and sulphurous gases. Lava may escape from the crater in the center or find its way out through vents in the side of the volcano, solidifying as it cools in the air. A major volcanic eruption can hurl boulders high into the air. These boulders, called *volcanic bombs*, can be very large in size. Pompeii and Herculaneum were both Roman towns that were buried under volcanic debris when Mount Vesuvius erupted in 79 A.D. The two towns are still being excavated today.

HOW DOES RAIN FALL?

There is always water vapor in the air. During the summer, there is more because the temperature is higher. When there is so much water vapor in the air, it only takes a tiny drop in temperature to make the vapor condense and form tiny droplets of water. Then, we say the air is saturated.

So, what happens when all these water droplets in a cloud meet a mass of cooler air? If the air is moist, the droplets cannot evaporate. Instead, they get bigger and bigger as more and more condensation takes place. Soon, each tiny droplet has become a drop, and it starts to fall downward. Then, we have rain!

FACT FILE

A rainbow is quite simply a great curved spectrum, or band of colors, caused by the breaking up of light which has passed through raindrops.

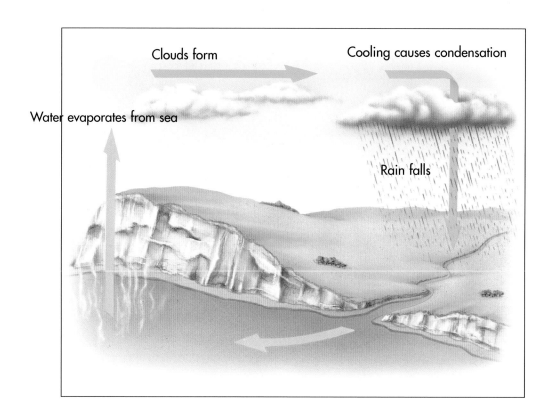

Clouds form

Cooling causes condensation

Water evaporates from sea

Rain falls

HOW DOES PRESSURE AFFECT OUR WEATHER?

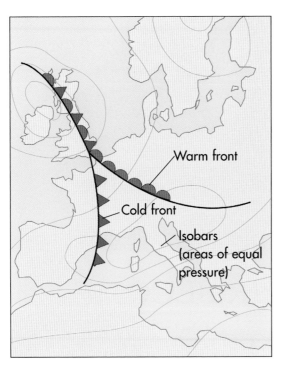

Warm front

Cold front

Isobars (areas of equal pressure)

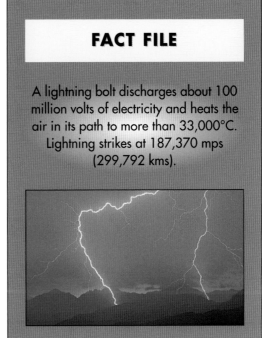

FACT FILE

A lightning bolt discharges about 100 million volts of electricity and heats the air in its path to more than 33,000°C. Lightning strikes at 187,370 mps (299,792 kms).

Weather is simply what the air or atmosphere is like at a given time. No matter what the air is–cold, cool, warm, hot, calm, breezy, windy, dry, moist, or wet–it is still weather.

Air pressure differs across all parts of the earth's surface, and this difference causes winds. Air will move from an area of high pressure, or an anticyclone, to an area of low pressure, or a depression.

Depressions are usually associated with bad weather conditions and rain. These changes in air pressure can be measured by an instrument called a *barometer*.

When the weather man talks about a weather front, he is referring to the boundary between two masses of air at different temperatures and pressures. With the use of computers, increasingly accurate forecasting is now available.

HOW DOES AIR BECOME POLLUTED?

Air pollution is caused mostly by human activities. Exhaust fumes from motor vehicles are one of the main pollutants. They contain greenhouse gases, which are thought to contribute to global warming. They also contain substances, such as sulphur and nitrogen oxides, that can cause damage to our lungs.

Large amounts of pollution are produced as a result of more and more industry. In many countries, industrial pollution is now controlled, but it still causes damage to our health and the environment in many developing countries.

Another recent form of pollution came from parts of Asia where large areas of the rainforest were burned to clear the land for farming.

FACT FILE

Deforestation can have a terrible effect on the ecology of a region.

HOW CAN AEROSOLS DAMAGE THE EARTH?

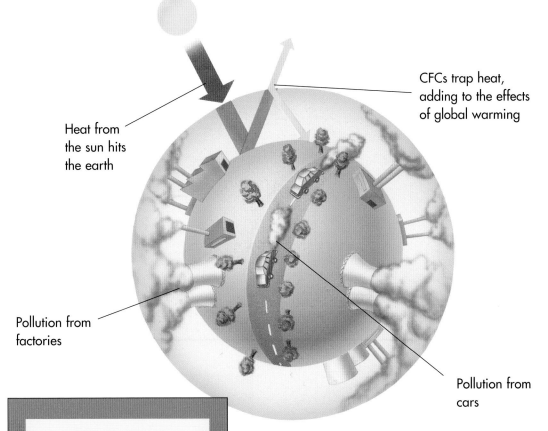

Heat from the sun hits the earth

CFCs trap heat, adding to the effects of global warming

Pollution from factories

Pollution from cars

FACT FILE

Mammoths lived in an area with a cool climate, but gradually the weather began to get warmer. Unable to adapt, the mammoth became extinct.

Scientists have discovered a gap in the protective ozone layer around the earth. The ozone, a form of oxygen, filters out more than 90 percent of the sun's harmful rays.

The hole in the ozone layer has been blamed on our use of chemicals called *chlorofluorocarbons* (or CFCs). They were widely used in refrigerators, freezers, and aerosol cans.

The use of CFCs has now been heavily restricted, but it may take many years before the ozone layer actually repairs itself.

WHEN ARE FUNGI EDIBLE?

Usually, the term "mushroom" is used to identify edible fungi. The term "toadstool" is often reserved for inedible or poisonous fungi. In a very restricted sense, the word "mushroom" indicates the common edible fungus of fields and meadows. Mushrooms have insignificant nutritive value. Their chief worth is as a specialty food of delicate, subtle taste and agreeable texture. Fungi can be found in damp areas or growing on tree trunks.

Poisoning by wild mushrooms is common and may be fatal. It may also produce merely mild gastrointestinal disturbance or a slight allergic reaction. It is important that every mushroom intended for eating is accurately identified before it is eaten.

FACT FILE

Fungi live on organic matter. In the soil, fungi are the most important agent in the breakdown of dead plant and animal material, recycling it so that plants can use the nutrients.

WHEN DO WE SEE FAIRY RINGS?

A fairy ring is a circular pattern that is produced by fungi growing in grassland. As the fungus grows out from a central point, it forms a circle. At the edges of this circle, the grass changes in appearance. Meanwhile, the original fungus dies off, so all that is left is the expanding ring of fungus

growing beneath the surface. Sometimes, a ring of mushrooms also appears. These fairy rings grow for many years, perhaps even for centuries. They can reach a large size unless they are disturbed.

FACT FILE

Fungi represent a separate kingdom of living things and should not be regarded as either plants or animals. There are thousands of different kinds of fungi, showing a huge variety of shape and lifestyle. The fungus kingdom is split into two divisions—slime molds and true fungi.

HOW WAS PENICILLIN DISCOVERED?

Penicillin was the first widely used antibiotic to be developed. It was discovered almost by accident by Sir Alexander Fleming in 1928. He was growing staphylococci bacteria on plates and neglected to wash them before he went on vacation. When he got back, he found that mold on the plates appeared to be killing the bacteria. However, he couldn't purify it to get enough to work with.

In the late 1930s, Ernest Chain, Howard Florey, and Norman Heatley worked to produce enough purified penicillin to test it. It worked on both mice and human beings. Production was started in America in 1941.

Penicillin has a powerful effect on some bacteria but not on others. Many bacteria are now becoming resistant to antibiotics that have been effective until now. So, researchers are looking for the next generation of treatments.

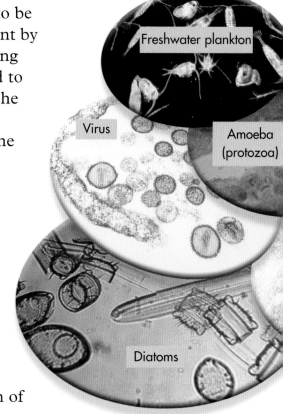

Freshwater plankton

Virus

Amoeba (protozoa)

Diatoms

FACT FILE

In 1347, a dreadful plague spread throughout London. Known as the "Black Death," this epidemic was caused by rats. It was very infectious, and spread rapidly, causing many thousands of deaths.

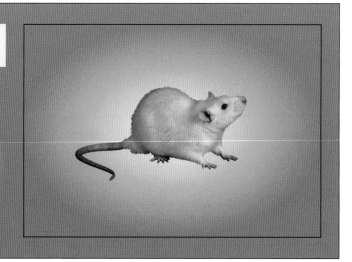

HOW DO BACTERIA AND VIRUSES DIFFER?

Amoeba

Bacteria

Influenza virus

Bacteria are the simplest living organisms. Unlike other living cells, bacteria do not have a nucleus. Their genes are scattered throughout their interior. Bacteria have a thick protective cell wall. There are thousands of bacteria in every single cubic meter of air that you breathe. Everything you touch is loaded with bacteria. They even live inside your body. Although bacteria can cause disease, the majority of them are completely harmless. They carry out the vital function of breaking down dead and waste materials. For example, bacteria in your stomach help the body to digest food.

Viruses are even smaller than bacteria, but strictly speaking, viruses are not alive. To be alive an organism must be able to grow and reproduce. Viruses cannot do this themselves, and the only way that they can reproduce is to enter a living cell and take control of it. This cell then becomes a living factory that can produce more viruses.

FACT FILE

Scientists are always looking for new cures for illnesses and diseases. Rainforests contain the bulk of the world's species of plants and trees. Each year, new plants are discovered and valuable plant chemicals are found. Hopefully, one day these will become a valuable source of medicine.

HOW DO PARASITES LIVE?

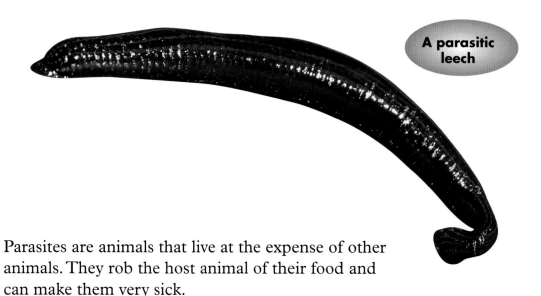

A parasitic leech

Parasites are animals that live at the expense of other animals. They rob the host animal of their food and can make them very sick.

The flea is a parasite that can be found on dogs, cats, and most other warm-blooded animals. It lives by sucking their blood.

However, in other relationships, different animals can help one another. Some hermit crabs, for example, place sea anemones on their shells, hiding under their protective stinging tentacles. At the same time, the sea anemone benefits because it shares the crab's food.

Similarly, a shrimp digs a burrow that it shares with the small goby fish. The fish benefits from being able to hide in the burrow, while acting as a lookout to warn the shrimp of approaching predators.

Most true parasites are very simple animals because they do not need complicated organs to digest their food. Indeed, some parasites are simply a mass of reproductive organs.

FACT FILE

Cleaner fish are tiny fish that live in coral reefs. They regularly clean parasites from much larger fish. Even large predatory fish need to to be cleaned of skin parasites. The cleaner fish can even swim into the predator's mouth without being eaten.

HOW ARE SWARMS OF LOCUSTS FORMED?

For thousands of years, locust swarms have devastated farmland throughout Asia and Africa. A swarm can be as large as 30 miles (50 km) long and can contain over 100,000 million locusts. A swarm of locusts can turn the sky totally black and wreak terrible damage on farmers' crops.

A locust is in fact a large grasshopper that normally lives a solitary and harmless existence. When their population builds up to a high level, they begin to mass together and migrate in search of food. These migrations can cover many thousands of miles.

FACT FILE

Other animals pack themselves closely together and move in unison as a herd. This makes it difficult for a predator to catch an individual animal.

WHAT IS POLLEN?

FACT FILE

Bees are attracted to the shape and scent of a flower. They feed on the nectar in the flower and gather pollen, which they store in sacs on their legs to take back to the hive.

Pollen is a plant's equivalent of an animal's sperm. It carries the male reproductive genes. Pollen consists of tiny grains, each with a tough coat that is often patterned with characteristic ridges and spikes. When inhaled, the fine pollen causes allergies, such as hay fever, in some susceptible people. Pollen can be found in fossil deposits, making it possible to identify the plants that were living in a certain time period even though no actual plant fossils may be found. Pollination takes place when a pollen grain is deposited on the tip of a pistil. It then grows a long tube down inside the pistil that fuses with the egg cell and completes the process of fertilization.

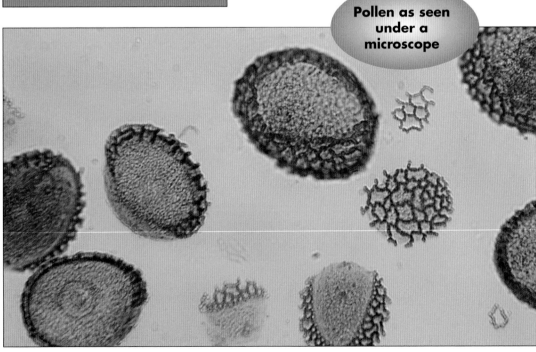

Pollen as seen under a microscope

WHAT ARE LICHENS?

Lichens are peculiar organisms in which algae and fungi live together. They are usually flat and crust-like with no roots. They often grow on roofs, rocks, or tree branches. Some grow like a small branched tree, while others can be found hanging from tree branches. The main structure of a lichen is the fungal part, but it also contains algae cells, which contribute food through photosynthesis. Lichens grow very slowly but can eventually cover very large areas. Some individual lichens are extremely old. Some lichens growing in rocks in Antarctica are thought to be 10,000 years old. They are the oldest living organisms.

FACT FILE

Reindeer moss is a form of lichen that is very common throughout the Arctic. It forms the main diet of caribou and other grazing animals.

WHAT IS AN INVERTEBRATE?

An invertebrate is an animal without a backbone. Invertebrates make up 97 percent of all animals. This group of animals includes all of the arthropods, such as spiders, insects, and crustaceans. The remaining invertebrates are soft-bodied animals, although many of them have shells. They include animals such as sponges, corals, shellfish, worms, sea urchins, starfish, and many less familiar animals. One invertebrate, the octopus, proved to be highly intelligent when it was studied in a laboratory. Experiments have shown that an octopus can recognize shapes and can remember different experiences.

Stag beetles

Tarantula spider

Earthworm

FACT FILE

Assassin bugs are well named. They attack other insects and suck out their body fluids. Caterpillars are a popular prey because they have soft bodies and often no means of defense.

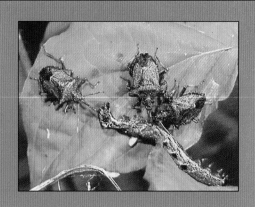

210

WHAT ARE ALGAE?

Algae are the most primitive form of plant life. Most algae are aquatic, and they can range in size from microscopic single-celled organisms to seaweed that is several feet long. Algae photosynthesize like other plants, and they are responsible for providing most of the world's oxygen. Algae structures are varied, but even the large forms, such as kelp, lack the true leaves, stems, and roots found in other plants. Not all algae use the green chlorophyll found in other plants in order to photosynthesize, some use red or brown pigments for this purpose.

FACT FILE

Giant kelp looks like a kind of seaweed, but it is in fact the largest kind of algae. It grows in very long strands up to 200 ft (65 m) in length and is fastened to the seabed with a root-like organ called a *holdfast*.

WHAT ARE PLANTS USED FOR?

Over thousands of years, human beings have found many uses for plants. Some of the most common ones are shown here:

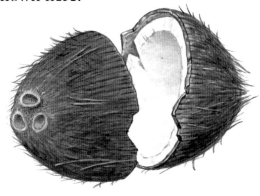

Coconut skins are used for making mats. Sisal and hemp also produce tough threads used for ropes and matting.

Most paper is made from the cellulose found in wood pulp.

FACT FILE

We also eat plants every day of our lives in one form or another.

Rubber comes from the sap of a tropical tree and is used for many things, including tires, boots, and erasers.

Many plant extracts are used to make medicines.

212

WHAT ARE UMBELS?

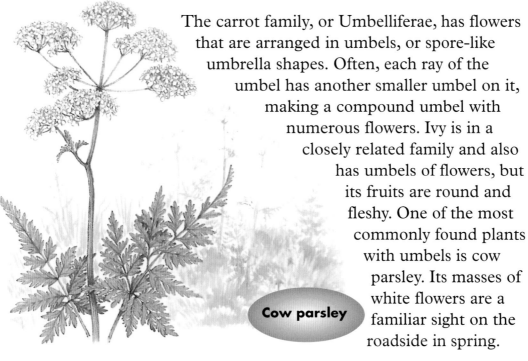

The carrot family, or Umbelliferae, has flowers that are arranged in umbels, or spore-like umbrella shapes. Often, each ray of the umbel has another smaller umbel on it, making a compound umbel with numerous flowers. Ivy is in a closely related family and also has umbels of flowers, but its fruits are round and fleshy. One of the most commonly found plants with umbels is cow parsley. Its masses of white flowers are a familiar sight on the roadside in spring.

Cow parsley

FACT FILE

Some of our familiar vegetables, such as parsnip and carrot, have been developed from wild plants of this family.

Ivy

WHAT IS CONSERVATION?

Conservation is planned management of nature so that it is not exploited or neglected. Over the last few decades, very large areas of natural habitats, once rich in plant and animal life, have disappeared under buildings, roads, and farms. The modern farming methods of large fields, intensive use of pesticides, and high crop yields do not give many wild flowers and animals a chance to survive. Nowadays, most species survive in places where these changes have not taken place–old woodland areas, for example. However, natural habitats are disappearing quickly, and constant effort is needed to conserve what is left. Reforestation efforts to replace trees used for lumber is one way conservation is seen. Without these efforts, plants and animal life may deteriorate so much that they become unsuitable for the species that depend on them for survival.

FACT FILE

A few plants are now so rare that they have become valuable. Some collectors or dealers attempt to dig up the rarest plants, such as orchids, so that they can sell them. Conservation organizations may erect special cages to protect these flowers.

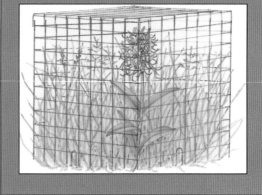

WHAT IS A CRUSTACEAN?

Crab

FACT FILE

People in many parts of the world eat lobsters, crabs, shrimps, and other crustaceans.

Crustaceans are aquatic arthropods such as crabs, lobsters, and shrimps. They have a very tough, jointed external skeleton and jointed walking legs. Their body is divided into a region that contains most of the internal organs, covered by a shell called the *carapace*, and a muscular tail section that is usually folded under the body. Many crustaceans have powerful pincers that they use to capture and break apart their prey. They also use their pinchers to signal to others of their species. Crustaceans live in sea and freshwater habitats. Many small crustaceans feed on plankton. These crustaceans are often eaten by larger fish, and even whales. Crustaceans form an important link between the small food-producing organisms and the larger animals in the aquatic food chain.

Lobster

WHAT IS A MARSUPIAL?

Marsupials are mammals. Unlike placental mammals, who bear young in a physically advanced state nourished through the exchange of nutrients and wastes through the placenta, most marsupial babies are born as embryos. They develop in their mother's pouch, attached to a nipple. They will remain in the pouch until they are fully developed and resemble a miniature adult. However, they will still be dependant on their mothers for milk and protection.

Opossum

Marsupials are native to North and South America and Australasia. The largest marsupials are the kangaroos and wallabies. Other well-known examples include wombats, koalas, and opossums. The extinct Tasmanian tiger was a marsupial. While many marsupials are vegetarian, some do eat invertebrates and insects.

Kangaroo

FACT FILE

The young of tree-dwelling marsupials, such as koalas and opossums, cling to their mother's back after they have left the pouch. They are small and at risk of falling from trees or being attacked by males.

WHAT IS A REPTILE?

Lizard

A reptile is an air-breathing animal with a body structure comprising traits of an amphibian, bird, and mammal. Reptiles are generally scaly, and their eggs are fertilized internally. Living reptiles include crocodiles, tortoises and turtles, snakes, and lizards. There are about 6,000 surviving species. Long ago, there were many more kinds of reptile, such as the dinosaurs and the flying pterosaurs. Most reptiles lay eggs or give birth to live young, which can then immediately live independent from the mother.

FACT FILE

The tortoise and turtle are the only reptiles with a shell. They pull their heads, legs, and tails into their shells, which serve as suits of armor. Few other backboned animals have such excellent natural protection.

Crocodile

WHAT IS A PECKING ORDER?

A living animal must behave in a manner that enables its survival. All animals are faced with the same basic problems. Animals do whatever they can to acquire all the energy they need for survival. In this basic sense, each animal is competing with all the other animals for this energy. Among animals that live in groups, one animal becomes the leader. In chickens, this means that one bird dominates all of the other birds.

The next one down in the "pecking order" can dominate all except the leader, and so on, until the bird at the bottom of this process can be bullied by the entire flock. This sort of "pecking order" is also evidenced in other animal groups.

FACT FILE

Dog fights do not usually cause much damage. The losing dog will usually submit by lying down, which reduces the level of aggression in the dominant dog.

meat-eater

grazing animal

dung fertilizes the soil

nutrients are absorbed by the plant

WHAT IS THE FOOD CHAIN?

FACT FILE

In overpopulated areas, people commonly increase the total food supply by cutting out one step in the food chain. Instead of consuming animals that eat cereal grains, the people themselves consume the grains.

A food chain is a sequence that demonstrates how one organism forms the food for another. It begins with the simplest animals and plants and continues until the top of the chain is reached. Human beings or predator animals are often at the top of food chains.

Plants, such as grass and trees, are towards the bottom of the food chain. Grazing animals eat these plants, and these animals are in turn eaten by predators, such as lions. Their dung fertilizes the soil, encouraging the growth of more plants. So, the food chain actually becomes a complete circle.

219

WHAT ARE NETTLES?

FACT FILE

The nettle family includes a diversity of plant types that range from small herbaceous species to large trees. Among the members are stinging nettles; mulberry, fig, and elm trees; hop vines; and hemp.

The nettle family is comprised of about 45 different species of herbs, shrubs, small trees, and a few vines, distributed primarily in tropical regions. Many species, for example the stinging nettle (or urtica), have stinging hairs on their stems and leaves. The leaves are varied, and the sap is usually watery. The small, greenish flowers often form clusters in the leaf axils. Both male and female flowers develop on the same plant. The curled stamens of the male flowers straighten quickly as the flowers open, releasing the pollen. The dry, one-seeded fruit is often enclosed by the outer whorl of the flower cluster. The dead-nettles have leaves like the stinging nettles, but they have no sting. The main characteristic of this large family are the square stems, opposite leaves, and whorls of irregular flowers.

Yellow archangel

Dandelion

WHAT IS A WEED?

Weeds are unwanted plants. They ruin crops by outgrowing them early in the season and outcompeting them for water, light, and nutrition. Poisonous weeds, such as ragwort, cause severe problems if they get into straw intended for animal feed or bedding. Some types of weeds shelter insects and diseases that damage nearby crops. In gardens, plants, such as bindweed, ground elder, and Japanese elder, are pernicious weeds and extremely difficult to get rid of. However, some weeds are beneficial to wildlife, providing food for caterpillars and shelter and seeds for birds.

FACT FILE

Weeds, like most wild plants, can also be beneficial. Dandelions can be eaten in salads and stinging nettles in tasty soups. Fireweed, one of many weeds used in making medicines, relieves pain.

WHAT IS THE TALLEST TREE IN THE WORLD?

The Californian giant redwood is one of the oldest and largest living organisms on earth. They often exceed 300 ft. (90 m) in height, and their trunks reach typical diameters of 10 to 20 ft. (3 to 6 m). The redwood tree takes 400 to 500 years to reach maturity, and some trees are known to be more than 1,500 years old. These ancient trees have very few branches and leaves and are often scarred by fire and lightning strikes. As the tree ages, the lower limbs fall away, leaving a clear, columnar trunk.

Californian giant redwood

FACT FILE

The oldest-known trees are bristlecone pine trees. They grow in the White Mountains in California. Although they are quite small, some of these gnarled trees are more than 4,500 years old.

WHAT ARE MUSSELS?

Mussels are mollusks and are related to water snails. Because their shells are divided into two halves, they are called *bivalves*. The shell protects the soft body of the animal. A powerful foot enables the animal to change its position. Mussels suck in water and extract the oxygen and food that they require from it. There are both marine and fresh water mussels, and they can be found worldwide. The marine mussels prefer cool seas. Freshwater mussels, also known as naiads, inhabit streams, lakes, and ponds. There are around 1,000 known species. The shells are dark blue or dark greenish brown on the outside, and on the inside, they have a pearly appearance. Mussels attach themselves to solid objects or to one another by strands called *byssus threads*. Mussels often appear in dense clusters.

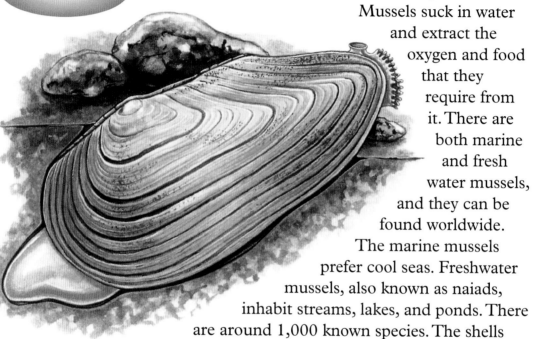
Swan mussel

FACT FILE

The oystercatcher is a bird that feeds largely on mollusks (such as mussels, clams, and oysters). They attack them as the tide ebbs, when their shells are exposed and still partially open.